TEN BOYS WHO CHANGED THE WORLD

LIGHT KEEPERS

Irene Howat

CF4·K

Copyright © 2001 Christian Focus Publications
Reprinted 2002, 2003, 2004, 2005 twice, 2007, 2008, 2010,
2011, 2012, 2015, 2016, 2017 (twice) and 2019
Paperback ISBN: 978-1-85792-579-1
epub ISBN: 978-1-84550-838-3
mobi ISBN: 978-1-84550-839-5

Published by Christian Focus Publications,
Geanies House, Fearn, Tain, Ross-shire
IV20 1TW, Scotland, Great Britain

www.christianfocus.com
email:info@christianfocus.com
Cover design by Alister MacInnes
Cover illustration by Elena Temporin,
Milan Illustrations Agency.
Printed and bound in Turkey

All incidents retold in these stories are based on true situations. Where specific information about childhood incidents has been unobtainable the author has written these paragraphs using other information concerning family life, hobbies, home life, relationships freely available in other biographies as well as appropriate historical source material.

Front cover: Brought up in Scotland, Eric Liddell practised running for the Olympics in the glens and valleys of his native land. This picture depicts Eric's unique running style where he would wave his arms enthusiastically.

For Helen and Elsie

Contents

Contents

Brother Andrew

Andrew crept along the dark side of the hedge, stopping only long enough to look behind him into the night to listen for any sounds that would warn him he was being followed. All he heard was the hooting of an owl in the wood near the village. He crept on.

A shaft of light fell across the footpath where there was a break in the hedge. The boy edged towards the gap, pulling his balaclava down over his face so that anyone looking out of the window wouldn't see him. Slowly, so slowly, Andrew leant forward, glanced at the window and sighed with relief. Although the light was on, there didn't seem to be anyone in the room, at least not at the window end. He darted round the hedge and out of the shaft of light. Only a few more steps and he'd know if it was there. As he edged his way along the side of the house, Andrew kept his ears open for any sound from inside, and his hands out in front of him to feel for it. Suddenly it was there! First one hand then another came in touch with the cold metal of bicycle handlebars.

The boy knelt down, every bit of him as tense as a cat about to spring, and felt over the bike. Was it tied to a drainpipe? Was there a chain that would stop it moving? There didn't seem to be. Taking a long piece of string from his pocket – it had been put there specially for the purpose – Andrew passed it from side to side along the back of the bike until he was absolutely sure that it was not attached to anything. Then he sat down and leant against the wall. He knew what he had to do. But he was scared ... scared half out of his mind.

Anger suddenly filled every part of him. And the anger of a twelve year old can be terrifically powerful. 'What right has he to work for the Germans?!' he demanded of himself. 'How can a Dutchman work for the enemy?! He's a traitor! All of his family are traitors! Well, he'll find it harder to do his dirty work without his bike!' Stuffing his hankie into the bell so that it would be absolutely silent, and taking off the chain to prevent it click-clicking as it moved, Andrew retraced his steps, this time with the bike beside him. Through the shaft of light he went, knowing that if he was caught he might not see his family again, round the hedge into the blissful darkness, then down the road to safety. Only when he was in the wood did Andrew replace the chain, take the hankie from the bell to wipe the sweat from his face, and mount the bicycle. There was not a sweeter moment in his life till then, when he braked at the school, ringing the bell for all he was worth. A member of the Dutch resistance opened the door to see what the noise was.

'Well done!' the man said, slapping the boy on the back. 'You're doing a man's job, Andrew. The war will be won by the likes of you.'

And that's what Andrew was in the middle of, a war, the Second World War.

Suddenly Andrew was surrounded by men, and they were all talking.

'That traitor will be useless without his bike!' one said.

'And we can put it to good use for the cause,' added another.

But it was what the third man said that thrilled the boy. 'You're a natural for the underground, son, a natural!'

The kind of cleverness that Andrew used for the resistance he also used to get out of attending church. Because his father was deaf, the family sat in the short front seat. Sunday by Sunday he would lag behind so that he was the one for whom there was no room. 'I'll have to sit at the back again !'

he'd moan, moving quickly to the rear of the church before anyone offered to swop with him. Then during the first hymn he was off, coming back only when he knew the service was about to end.

It probably didn't come as a surprise to anyone when Andrew decided to be a soldier, although it made his mother very sad. The Second World War was by then over, and he was posted not to the German border, but to Indonesia. As a boy, he had been really scared when he was working for the resistance, but as a soldier he thought he was invincible. He came to believe that whoever was hit by a bullet, it certainly wouldn't be him. But Andrew was wrong. And the bullet that went right through his ankle, left him crippled for a time. He was just twenty years old.

'Do you want this?' the nurse in the army hospital asked, when he had begun to recover from surgery. She had a Bible in her hand. 'It was in your kit.'

Andrew looked at the Bible his mother had given him when he joined the army. He hadn't opened it once, and he didn't want to look at it now. He was angry with God, if there was a God. But hospitals can be boring places, and eventually he was bored into reading his mother's Bible.

'I think you should sleep for a while,' a young doctor said, finding his patient still reading hours later.

'I'm not tired,' Andrew replied. 'Have you ever read this?' he asked. 'I'd no idea it was interesting. It's like an adventure.'

'I suppose it depends which bit you read,' suggested the doctor.

Andrew looked puzzled. 'I started at the beginning. That's where books usually start.'

Between reading his Bible and writing to his seventy-two Dutch penpals, Andrew's time in hospital passed quite quickly. One of his penpals, a Christian girl called Thile, answered as best she could all his questions about the Bible.

In November 1949, Andrew left the army and was sent home. With part of his pay he bought a bicycle. 'I'd better buy one than steal one,' he thought, remembering back to his childhood.

'Is he all right?' his father asked over and over again after he returned home. 'He's either stuck in the Bible or he's cycling off to church services all over the place.'

Andrew's sister shook her head. 'I'm worried about him too. It's just not natural! Maybe the war has bent his mind.'

'I don't know about that,' Father said. 'I think it's his way of coping with being crippled. But I hope he grows out of it. Nobody likes people who are too religious.'

Andrew didn't grow out of it. Not very long after coming back home from Indonesia, he discovered for himself that the Bible was true. The former underground boy and soldier found new life in Jesus. And as he wondered about his future, Andrew's prayer was, 'Lord, show me what you want me to do with my life.'

God did show Andrew what he wanted him to do, and he also showed him that his childhood experience of the Dutch resistance, during wartime, was good training for Christian service.

Brother Andrew (that's what he became known as) found himself working as a smuggler for God. After the Second World War, many communist countries banned the Bible. It was as though a line - it was known as the Iron Curtain - was drawn across Europe. On the western side, people were free to come and go, to be Christians or Muslims or nothing at all. On the eastern side, behind the Iron Curtain, men and women were not free to travel, not free to have Bibles, not even free to teach their own children about the Lord. It was for those people that Brother

Andrew became a smuggler, taking Bibles and other Christian books and tracts to people who could be put in prison if they were found in possession of them.

'I can hardly take in all that the Lord has done in the ten years since I became a Christian,' Brother Andrew said to his companion. 'Take this car, for example. Do you want to know how I got it?'

His friend nodded then listened to the story.

'A couple I knew heard about the work I was doing, smuggling Bibles and tracts behind the Iron Curtain. They realised that I could take much larger quantities if I had a car. And they know I don't walk well and thought it would make my job a whole lot easier. I was in West Berlin when I phoned to tell them my plans. "You'd better come right back here for the keys," my old friend told me. "What keys?" I asked. I remember him chuckling at the end of the phone. "We've got you a car," my friend said. "If you come for the keys, you can drive it all the way to Moscow if you dare." I went right back, collected the car and tucked as many boxes of Bibles in it as I could!'

'Is that why you call it the miracle car?' the young man asked.

Brother Andrew laughed. 'That's one reason. Another is that it keeps on going!'

It was that same car that Brother Andrew was driving when he reached the Yugoslavian border one day. Drawing up at the checkpoint he prayed, 'Lord, I have Bibles in the car. When you were on earth, you made blind eyes see. Please make seeing eyes blind now, so that the guards don't see the Bibles.'

'Anything to declare?' the guard asked.

'My watch, money, camera ... only small things.'

He was telling the truth because the Bibles were small.

'We don't need to bother about them,' the guard said, handing Brother Andrew's passport back.

'Thank you for making them blind to the boxes!' he prayed, as he drove into Yugoslavia with his precious load. For the next seven weeks he was there and he held eighty meetings and gave out hundreds of Bibles and tracts.

Marta, a young Christian girl, was delighted to have a Bible of her own.

'Tell me about yourself,' Brother Andrew invited.

'I was brought up in a Christian home,' she said, 'and I became a Christian myself. At school I always said grace before my lunch. Because of that, I was expelled from school by the Communists. I was told I couldn't go back because I was filling the other pupils' heads with nonsense. But I'm a Christian, and I can't pretend I'm not. That would be denying Jesus.'

Brother Andrew prayed with Marta, asking God to give her strength and courage for the future.

The road was dusty as he left Marta's town. 'It's amazing this car doesn't seize up,' Brother Andrew said to Nikola, a Yugoslav believer, as the dust blew all around. 'You'd think the dust would get into the engine. I'm sure God stops that happening because we pray about it each morning.'

Nikola smiled. 'I'd never heard anyone praying over a car before I met you!'

As they drove along, a small lorry approached them from the opposite direction. It also had foreign number plates. When the drivers saw each other, they stopped to discuss the state of the road.

'You're Brother Andrew,' the other driver said. 'And this is the miracle car.'

Nikola grinned. 'All the Christians know him,' he thought. 'It's amazing the Communists haven't found out about him!'

'May I have a look at your car?' the lorry driver said. 'I'm a mechanic, and it wouldn't do any harm to give it a going over. You do so many miles.'

Having spent some time under the bonnet, the lorry driver scratched his head and looked puzzled.

'Is there anything wrong?' Brother Andrew asked.

'No,' the man answered, 'the car's going well. But I can't work out how it can go at all. The carburettor is clogged, so are the spark plugs. And the air filter is totally clogged up. This car should have ground to a standstill thousands of miles ago!'

Setting to, the mechanic unclogged the carburettor and spark plugs and did what he could about the air filter. Then he tuned the engine and changed the oil.

'Look after it,' he told the two men. 'It's a miracle car so don't abuse it.'

And it was just as big a miracle meeting a Christian mechanic on a lonely road in Yugoslavia, and one who knew Brother Andrew! God provided a mechanic for the car, he provided the car for Brother

Andrew, and through that Dutch Christian, the Lord provided Bibles and tracts to many thousands of people who would otherwise not have been able to read God's Word for themselves.

FACT FILE

Communism: Communism was the form of government which existed on the eastern side of the Iron Curtain.

State control extended to all parts of society, and individual freedom was restricted. Newspapers and books had to follow the communist line, and religious beliefs were discouraged.

Communism in eastern Europe lasted until 1989, when it finally fell and brought the Berlin wall down with it. Movement across borders was no longer restricted, and freedom of worship was restored.

Keynote: God miraculously provided Brother Andrew with a car, a mechanic who could fix it and thousands of Bibles and tracts. These were smuggled behind the Iron Curtain and given to people who would otherwise never have been able to read about Jesus.

Learn from how God amazingly provided for Brother Andrew. See God's hand in everything. Believe that he can bring about miracles in your life too.

Think: Have you ever thought about how wonderful it is to be free to read the Bible in your own language?

Pray for missionaries involved in translating the Bible and bringing it to people who have never been able to read it before.

 Prayer: Lord Jesus, thank you for how wonderfully you have provided for me. Thank you for my Bible. Help me to treasure it more than I do.

Bless those who are trying to bring your Word to people who have never been able to have their own Bibles. Amen.

John Newton

The ship's boy ran to the rail to see Liverpool disappear into the distance. He waved to the shore and wondered if anyone was waving back. Then he got to work, tidying the coils of rope on the deck. The rope was heavy with sea water, and his arms struggled with the weight of it. But the weight that was bothering John was not the wet rope, it was the feeling he had of carrying a heavy stone where his heart should have been.

'What's your name, lad?' a deckhand asked, as he helped the boy with the rope.

'John Newton, sir.'

The deckhand smiled. Not many people called him 'sir'! 'And what age are you?'

'I'm nine, sir.'

The man thought about his own son, who was almost the same age. 'Did your mother not think you were too young to be at sea?' he asked.

'My mother's dead, sir. And my stepmother doesn't seem to think I'm too young. I'm strong for my age,' John said defiantly.

The deckhand looked the lad up and down. 'I can see that,' he said. 'You certainly are a strong young man. What about your father? Doesn't he mind you being at sea?'

'My father's a sea captain, sir.'

And there was no arguing with that.

That night, as John curled up in the corner where the ship's boys slept, he thought about his mother. She had loved her little son, and his heart was broken when she died. Now all he had to remember her by were her stories, most of them about Jesus.

The boy tried to tell himself one of her stories, but, before he got to the end of it, he was sound asleep. Sea air and hard work had exhausted him.

If that first night at sea was bad, there was a very much worse one to follow five years later, in 1739.

'I'm going for a drink,' John, told his friends. He thought he was very grown up. 'Anyone else coming?'

Nobody was.

'Why's that man watching me?' the teenager wondered, as he drank his rum. 'I'm sure I've never seen him before.'

Because the man's gaze made him feel uncomfortable, John left as soon as he had finished his drink.

'Stop!' a voice said, from just beside him.

Fear ran through his veins, and John sprinted away as fast as he could. Several footsteps followed his. The boy's mind raced as fast as his feet. 'It's a press gang ... I've got to get out of here!'

But the footsteps were getting closer and louder. John dodged up an alley and raced for all he was worth. His lungs felt as though they were bursting.

'Gotcha!' spat a voice, as he was grabbed by the coat.

The boy struggled, but two sets of strong arms held him and swung him round. He was face to face with the staring man from the public house.

'That was a fair try,' the man gasped, for he too was winded. 'But the King wants you on board.'

John didn't need to be told any more. He knew he had been press-ganged into the King's navy. He'd be lucky if he stood on dry land again for months.

Although John Newton knew he couldn't do a thing about it, he didn't go willingly. He was half dragged, half carried to the man-of-war where he was held tightly while the hatch to the hold was opened. Then he was thrown into the darkness below. John didn't have long, and he knew it.

'Psst!' he said, holding some pennies through a fine grill in the roof of the hold each time he heard feet passing overhead.

The other men and boys who had been press-ganged jeered. 'You'll not buy yourself out with two pence!' one said, amid ugly laughter.

'What are you wanting?' a voice asked through the grill eventually.

'Take this,' John Newton said, 'and tell the Lieutenant I want to speak to him. My name's Newton.'

'That was a right waste of money!' a prisoner laughed in the darkness.

But John fared better than the others. The Lieutenant did come, and when he discovered that the boy's father was a captain, John was taken out of the hold and given a job as a midshipman. But his promotion didn't last long. John tried to jump ship and was caught. When HMS *Harwich* set sail, he was an ordinary seaman. And when he got the chance to change ships,

John was off, this time not to a naval boat, but to a merchant ship, *Pegasus*, and the cargo it normally carried was slaves.

With its hold full of drink and silks and other goods, the ship set sail for West Africa, for the Gulf of Guinea. And when they docked there, the hold was emptied of its cargo which was used to barter for slaves.

'That's a fine one,' the captain said looking at a tall young African. Then he saw another black man. 'I'll take him too.' A shorter, thinner man was pushed forward. 'He's not worth having.' The man was shoved back and a strong-looking young woman thrust forward. 'I'll take her,' shouted the captain. 'Put her on.'

John Newton watched as their cargo was loaded. Men were thrown into one hold, women and children into another. They were manacled together, and any who struggled had iron collars locked around their necks and were fixed to the wooden side of the ship. The Africans were packed together so that they had no room to move, and their chains held them fast. Even the children were chained.

'We should get a good price for that lot,' John said, looking at the terrified cargo.

'Let's just hope they survive to be sold,' answered the captain. 'It's a long way across the Atlantic to America.

'How many went overboard today?' a sailor asked, as John added up the figures.

'Four,' he answered. 'One man, two women and a baby.'

'All dead of the fever?' inquired the sailor.

'Not the baby. Its screaming got on the captain's nerves.'

And the ship ploughed on through a stormy sea. The foul air in the hold was choking, and the movement of the ship turned the Africans in each hold into one lump of terrified and miserable humanity.

Those who survived were sold as slaves in America, and their lives there were no better than on board the ship. The longest a slave lived in the lime fields, even a young, strong man, was nine years.

The captain of *Pegasus* and John Newton became good friends, and they spent a lot of time together. But that didn't please the captain's island wife. And when John took ill with fever, she left him starving and without water. The captain, thinking his wife was looking after his friend, went inland.

Too weak to move, John lay nearly dying. There was a rustle at his side, and a hand reached out with a little food for him.

'Thank you,' Newton whispered weakly to the black slave.

A short time later another slave came, this time with water which he poured down Newton's throat. The Africans John had brought into slavery were the only ones who helped him.

For several days he lay there dreadfully ill, getting only the food and drink the slaves brought out of their pitiful rations. When the Captain came back, he believed the lies his wife told, and John was put out in the fields and set to work with the slaves.

It was only by smuggling a scrap of a note back to his father, that help came in the shape of Captain Manesty of the *Greyhound*, a ship on its way to Ireland.

And it was on that voyage, when a furious storm threatened to wreck the boat with the loss of all hands, that John Newton started thinking about the God of whom his mother had told him when he was a boy.

Slave trading was seen as a good career, and on John's next voyages, which he eventually made as captain, he tried to be less harsh on the people he carried to slavery, only putting them in iron neck collars if there was no other way of controlling them. He did have them all in wrist rings and chains though. His crew wouldn't have taken the ship out of port otherwise. But, while he didn't see it as a cruel trade, John's wife, Mary, did. They had married when he was on shore leave, and what he did for a living saddened her terribly.

On his final voyage, the horror of it all dawned on John Newton. Suddenly he saw the slaves as people. He saw the men as brothers and husbands and fathers. Looking at the women, he saw sisters and wives and mothers. And when he turned his eyes on the young slaves, he saw them for what they were: boys and girls, children.

Jesus kept coming into John Newton's mind. Things were happening to him that he wanted to understand but didn't. And he longed for the day he'd be home and able to talk them over with his wife.

'It's so good to be back,' he told Mary, hugging her tightly some months later. 'I can't tell you how good it is to be home.'

His wife smiled. 'I just wish I could keep you here. I've looked forward so much to the end of your voyage.'

John looked into her eyes. 'So have I,' he said. 'So have I.'

John had been a working man for twenty one years. He started as a ship's boy at nine, and he was now thirty, a captain and very happily married. His home leave was coming near its end when strong, fit, John Newton, suffered a stroke. It was a minor stroke, and he recovered well, but it marked the end of his life at sea.

While she was concerned about her husband's health, Mary was delighted to see the back of his involvement in the slave trade. And so was John, especially as he became a Christian a very short time after his illness. John was turned around from a life of unbelief to a life of following and trusting in God. John knew that from now on God would guide him, instruct him and teach him to become more like his Saviour, Jesus Christ. It was the year 1755.

'Mary, I really think the Lord is calling me to be a minister,' John told his wife, not long afterwards.

A thrill surged through her as she took in what he was saying.

'Do you think that's possible?' he asked. 'Could a slave trader become a minister?'

Mary could hardly trust herself to speak. But her shining eyes and her smile answered his question. And that's what John Newton did. He became a minister of the Church of England.

'Tell me more about the slave trade,' a young politician asked John Newton some years later. His name was William Wilberforce.

John smiled. 'When you first came to see me,' he said, 'you were more worried about your own sins than about the conditions of slaves.'

The young man's eyes lit up at the memory. 'That's true,' Wilberforce agreed. 'But you showed me that Jesus could take away my sins and throw them into the depths of the sea.'

The two men talked for hours, of being saved from their sins, and of the terrible sins of slavery.

Wilberforce was determined to use his political influence to change things. And he did. In 1807, an Act of Parliament abolished the slave trade. Having just heard that the Act had been given its Royal Assent, John Newton slipped into a coma and never regained consciousness. The last thing he heard on earth was that wonderful news. The next thing he heard was God's voice welcoming him home to heaven.

FACT FILE

Press-ganging: Press gangs were groups of tough navy petty officers and seamen who scoured English seaports for men to take to sea. Since there were never enough volunteers for the navy, these men were 'pressed' into service by force, as John Newton was.

Sometimes mayors of harbour towns supplied the press gangs with the men they needed by clearing out the prisons. Press-ganging ended in the early 1800s.

Keynote: God opened John's eyes to see his need of Jesus and the awfulness of the slave trade. It didn't stop there though. John's influence on his friend William Wilberforce ended the slave trade for good.

Learn from how God used John Newton to influence a politician and bring about a positive change in the world. Don't underestimate how God can use you and never be afraid to speak out for him.

Think: There are a lot of issues on which the Christian viewpoint needs to be heard in parliament, for example, abortion and religious education in schools. Why not write your local politician explaining how you feel about these issues?

Pray that Christians in the world of politics will be able to present the Christian view when decisions are made.

Prayer: Lord Jesus, thank you for Christians who are able to influence decision-making in this country. Give them the courage to speak up for you and help me to do the same. Amen.

Billy Graham

The horse easily made it over the jump, but the rider didn't. His descent started off as a wobble, went on to be a gentle slide, and finished as a splash into a muddy puddle. Billy picked himself up, shook the worst of the mud out of his hair and grinned at his horse which had stopped and made its way back to him. He remounted. 'I guess you and I have to keep Suzie in work,' he told the horse. 'We can't have her sitting around doing nothing all day!'

'Billy Graham!' Suzie, the maid, gasped. Her smiley eyes sparkled, and her strong arms, dark brown and weather-beaten, were placed firmly on her hips. 'What have you been doing? Did you think the laundry basket needed filling?'

The boy grinned. 'It wasn't my fault,' he explained, clapping his mount. 'This fellow just wanted to keep you busy, so he found the biggest puddle in the ranch and dumped me into it.'

'Well, come you down here and strip off.'

Suzie was a big woman, but even though he was just fifteen, Billy Graham was bigger. 'Six feet two in his socks,' his mother often said. Having peeled off his muddy clothes, he dumped them on the floor and headed to his room.

'I guess you'll be back with some sweaty baseball gear later,' Suzie said to his back as he closed the door.

'At least I'm predictable!' Billy laughed.

Suzie sang as she worked. The Grahams were good to work for. She liked the ranch and she liked the children, especially Jean, the little cutie who came along years after the other three. But she knew her place. 'Blacks and whites are different. Whites employ blacks; blacks work for whites. That is just a fact of life in the southern states of America. And I'm not complaining,' muttered Suzie to herself. 'There's a lot worse off than me.'

'Still at it?' Billy asked, as he passed through the kitchen on his way out.

The maid laughed and lifted a still muddy shirt from even more muddy water. 'You did it good and proper,' said Suzie, 'so I've got to do it good and proper too. Are you riding to school?'

'Yeh! I sure am!'

'Well, you mind that puddle, Billy Graham, you just mind that puddle.'

The gangly youth sang as he rode. It was baseball night, and he wanted to be a pro. The fact that he wasn't a great player didn't seem to matter to him. He enjoyed the game and that was enough for Billy. In fact, he just enjoyed life.

'Your dad's had an accident, and your mom's gone with him to the hospital,' Suzie told Billy, when he came home that evening.

The boy sank on to a chair. 'What happened?'

'He was using the mechanical saw in the barn when a piece of wood flew out of the saw and smashed his head open.'

His eyes searched hers for the truth. 'Is it serious?'

He saw the answer in Suzie's eyes.

'Is he ... going to die?' Suddenly the six-foot-two teenager looked and sounded like a little boy. What he most wanted to do was cry and have Suzie's big arms round him. But he was too old for that now; he was trying to be a man.

'He's hurt real bad,' she said, 'and I've not stopped praying since it happened.'

'Keep praying,' Billy said urgently. At the same time he knew that he wouldn't be praying. What good would that do?

It looked as though Mr Graham was going to die. His doctors certainly expected him to. But Mrs Graham, who had just started to attend a Bible class three weeks before the accident, called all her friends and asked them to pray. She was utterly convinced that the Lord would hear their prayers and heal her husband. And that's what happened. From then on Billy's father and mother took their faith seriously, which was more than he did. He reckoned it was rubbish.

'Time to get up, Billy!' Mrs Graham shouted. 'It's half past five!'

The boy rolled over, stretched, and hoisted himself out of bed. He was hardly awake when he reached the kitchen, where a steaming mug of coffee and brown bread with maple syrup were laid out for him.

'Why can't we fix cows' body clocks so that they can be milked when it's light instead of at quarter to six in the morning.'

His mother laughed. 'Dad's working on that,' she said. 'But it's not coming quickly!'

A short sprint down to the cowshed and Billy slipped into the milking routine. He enjoyed this time of day. After the cold air, he loved the warm smell of the cows, the playful flick of their tails, and their deep pools of brown eyes. And there was no drink sweeter to him than the frothy milk that drained through the corrugated cooler. The mug he had when he finished milking, left him with a white moustache. He was usually wiping it off with his sleeve when he went back into the kitchen to Suzie, and his post-milking breakfast.

'There are Christian meetings on these evenings,' Mr Graham said. 'Want to come?'

Billy shook his head firmly. 'No way!'

But he changed his mind when one of his friends assured him that the preacher was no cissy; he was a real man's man.

Billy did go, and he went back again. One night something happened that changed his life. There were no cissy stories, just hard-hitting facts about man's sin - about Billy's sin - and about his need for a Saviour.

'Would anyone who wants to become a Christian move to the front,' the preacher said.

And Billy Graham, who thought Christianity wasn't for him, got to his feet and went to the front. That night he trusted himself to the Lord Jesus Christ.

Two years later, in 1937, when Billy was nineteen years old, he went to Bible School. It was there that he first spoke at a meeting. All he did was tell what the Lord had done for him. There was nothing special about how he spoke. He wasn't dramatic, wasn't memorable. There was nothing whatever that night to show that, before the end of his life, he would preach to over forty million people, in hundreds of different countries. His first congregation had no way of knowing that hundreds of thousands of people would become Christians as a result of Billy Graham crusades. And if they'd been told that would happen, they would probably not have believed it.

It was in the 1940s that Billy became known as a conference speaker, and, before long, invitations were coming thick and fast.

'Will you come to Los Angeles?'

'Would you consider a crusade in England?'

'Here's an invitation to go to Australia.'

The crusade team which Billy formed had its work cut out.

In the fifties, radio broadcasts and television appearances took his voice and his face into homes all over America and beyond.

'Have you heard Billy Graham?' people asked, not 'Have you heard of Billy Graham?' Everyone had.

During the 1960s, America was torn apart on the subject of race. Black children were taken miles by bus to black schools, where there would not be one single white pupil. There were separate churches, separate shopping areas, separate housing estates. American blacks and whites did not mix. And when efforts were made to break down the race barrier, fighting broke out at school gates, bombs were placed in churches, and people were maimed and killed. It was an ugly time in American history.

Billy Graham had grown up with Suzie, the black maid. He was brought up in a culture of white masters and black servants. And it wasn't until after he was converted that he realised the wrongness of it all. Billy's crusade team was one of the first major American organisations to have black and white members working together as equals.

'Would you consider speaking in Birmingham, Alabama?' Billy Graham was asked. 'Terrible things have been happening there. Worst of all, four children were killed in the bombing of a black church. Only the love of God can cut through that kind of hatred.'

Graham agreed to go, insisting that there be much prayer in the run-up to his visit.

'Look at that!' said the man who had issued the invitation. 'See what God's doing.'

It was Easter Sunday 1964, and the two men were standing in front of a crowd in a vast stadium.

'There are 30,000 people here,' he went on. 'They're about half-and-half black and white.' The man's eyes shone with joy and tears.

And they're sitting together side by side,' Billy smiled, 'just as they'll do in heaven.'

Billy preached his heart out that night in Alabama. And when he invited people to come forward, black and white came together, actually touching each other as they walked out to the front and stood together before the Lord. White men explained the gospel to black men, black women prayed with white women. God's love broke through man's hatred in Birmingham, Alabama.

When Billy Graham was a boy, his world was southern America, and he wasn't much interested in anywhere else. Years later, his vision stretched right round the globe as he travelled from country to country, continent to continent, telling anyone who would come to listen, that God loved sinners enough to die for them. He told ordinary men and women from backgrounds like his own. He could talk in a way that cowhands understood. He had been a cowhand himself. But he could also talk to presidents and to kings and queens, telling them that they, too, were sinners, that there was a King of Kings they would meet one day, who would judge them.

FACT FILE

The First World War: The First World War ended in 1918, the year Billy was born. There had been a terrible loss of life. Millions of young men died, many of them in the trenches, which were ditches dug deep into the ground.

The trenches were meant to shelter soldiers from enemy gunfire, but they offered little protection from the shells which exploded overhead. Soon they filled up with mud, water, rats and dead bodies. Many soldiers drowned in them or died from disease.

Keynote: At first Billy didn't see the point of praying and going to hear about Jesus at a Christian meeting. It was the last thing he wanted to do. But God changed all that!

Billy came to love Jesus, became convinced about the power of prayer and went on to share Jesus with millions.

Learn from how God turned Billy's life around and believe that

God can reach and use even those who have no time for him.

Think: God lifted Billy's eyes beyond his homeland, giving him a vision for the world. He wanted to take the message of Jesus around the globe.

Pick seven different countries across the world (one for every day of the week) and find out more about them. Pray for these countries each week - for the people, the Christians and the missionaries.

Prayer: Lord Jesus, thank you for showing me that prayer is powerful.

Help me to believe that, as I pray for countries across the world, my prayers can make a difference. Amen.

Eric Liddell

Robbie and Eric raced round the table, but the stray kitten could run faster than they could. She dodged under the table and came out the other side, but the boys had to stop and move the chairs. Their mother, Mrs Liddell, came in to see what the noise was, though it wasn't unusual for the boys to run helter-skelter round the table. Eric always seemed to be running somewhere.

'Kitten likes our home!' three-year-old Eric wailed, as the end of a tail disappeared round the door.

Robbie, who was a year-and-a-half older, decided this was the time to bring up the subject of pets ... yet again.

'Why can't we have a kitten like this one?' he asked.

Eric stopped crying. 'Me want a dog.'

Mrs Liddell sat down to talk to the boys, explaining to them for the hundredth time that in China there was a disease called rabies, and that animals who caught rabies could pass it on to people.

'But the people would get better,' Robbie said.

'No,' his mother told him. 'Often they die. That's why we can't have a cat or dog.'

The boys didn't give up, and neither did their little sister when she was old enough to know what was going on. Eventually, Mr and Mrs Liddell decided that they would adopt a family of goats who lived near them.

'The billy goat's mine,' Robbie said proudly.

'My goat's the nanny,' announced Eric.

And Jenny, their little sister, helped look after the kid.

'Run for it!' Eric yelled in Chinese, as the billy goat raced after them.

Robbie's pet was turning out to be quite an aggressive creature. All three ran as fast as they could, though it wasn't easy for them to get up much speed as they were dressed in traditional thickly-padded Chinese clothes. But at least the padding meant that if they were butted by Billy, it wasn't as sore as it might have been!

'You're getting faster and faster every time he chases you,' Mr Liddell told Eric one day. 'But you run in the funniest way. Your arms seem to go in every direction apart from the right one!'

But Eric wasn't always able to run.

'He's lost so much weight,' Mrs Liddell said, looking at him, pale and thin in bed. 'He's never been as poorly as this before.'

Mr Liddell shook his head. 'I'm so glad you're a nurse,' he added. 'We might have lost him otherwise. And he seemed to be recovering as well as the other two at first.'

'It's strange,' his wife thought aloud. 'He's such an active boy, but when he's ill, he goes down like a ton of bricks.'

Eric's eyes opened. 'Would you like a drink?' Mrs Liddell asked.

The boy nodded, and she held a cup of meat juice to his lips. That was all he was able to take.

'That boy will never be able to run again,' a pessimistic and insensitive visitor said, when she saw Eric two weeks later.

Mrs Liddell winked at her son so the visitor couldn't see. 'I'm quite sure he will,' she said, continuing to massage his stiff legs. 'He'll learn to walk again very soon, and before long he'll be out playing football with his friends.'

Eric looked down at his spindly legs. 'Would he walk again?' he wondered, especially as his knees didn't want to bend at all. Then he thought about his mother. 'Sure I will,' he decided. 'Mum's a nurse so she knows best.'

It took time, but Eric did walk again, and he did run, and he did play football.

'Will you come and play at my house on Sunday?' one of Eric's Chinese friends asked.

Eric shook his head. 'May I come on Saturday instead?'

'Why?'

'Christians believe that Sunday is God's special day, and we do different things on Sundays than on other days.'

The Chinese boy looked puzzled. 'Like what?'

'Well, we go to church, and we read Christian books, and we play Bible games, and we have a special dinner ... lots of things like that. It's a really good day.'

'Is that just because your dad's a missionary?'

'No,' explained Eric. 'It's because God's law tells us to keep Sunday special.'

His friend shrugged his shoulders. 'I suppose you'd better come on Saturday then.'

And that Saturday, the two boys organised a sports day for their friends.

Like many missionary children at that time (Eric was born in 1902) the boys came back to Britain for their education. After school in London, both Robbie and Eric went to Edinburgh University. Eric studied science, but his two great passions were his faith in the Lord Jesus and his running, even if his arms still went in every direction but the right one! And in 1924, he was making such good speeds that he was chosen to race in the Olympic Games!

'Liddell! Liddell! Liddell!' the university team screamed, as he reached the tape in a practice race.

The team manager looked at his stopwatch. 'Great!' he shouted. 'Your speed's getting better and better.'

Eric got his breath back. 'It's coming on for the 100 metres,' he said. 'But I only seem able to cope with that and the 200 metres. Any more than that and I just slow down.'

His coach smiled. 'We're pinning our hopes on you for the 100 metres,' he said. 'Anything else is a bonus.'

'The 100 metres heat is on Sunday ....' Eric was told.

'I'm not running on a Sunday,' he said quietly, but very firmly.

The Bible says that Sunday is special.

Those who knew Eric understood, even if they didn't agree with him. Others thought he was a traitor, letting his country down. Even some newspaper headlines were cruel. Instead of preparing for the 100 metres race, Eric trained for the 400 metres instead, even though he wasn't a distance runner.

Despite all the upset, the Games were exciting. Eric's British team-mate, Harold Abrahams, won the gold in the 100 metres, and Eric was right there at the tape to cheer him. His was the first British 100 metre gold ever. Then came the 200 metres. Harold, Eric and four Americans were running in the final. The two friends started well, but they couldn't keep up the speed. Harold fell behind. Eric just couldn't catch the top two Americans. The Scotsman's legs pounded on, reaching the tape in third place. He had won the bronze medal, equal to the best done by a British runner in the 200 metres at the Olympics. Things were going really well for the British team.

The 400 metres wasn't Eric's distance and his times over 400 metres were nothing special at all, certainly not Olympic special. But, despite all that, he would run. Eric got through the first heat, and the second. He qualified for the semi-final, and got into the final. But what chance had he? In one of the heats, a Swiss runner ran the distance in 48 seconds, which was listed as the world record at the time. In one semi-final an American had clocked just under 48 seconds.

As the runners lined up for the final, a pipe band burst into the skirl of a Scottish tune, and, when the band finished, the runners crouched for the off. The starting pistol cracked, and Eric shot away in first position, running as though he was going for the 100 metres.

'He's away far too quickly!'

'He'll never keep that up!' his friends shouted to each other above the noise of the crowd.

Arms and legs going everywhere, Eric pounded on, past the 100 metres, still in the lead. The 200 metres mark came up and he hadn't slackened off. His head was back, he was racing blind, but on and on he went. At the 300 metres mark, an American was gaining speed and closing on Eric.

'He's slowing,' one of his team-mates moaned.

'He's tiring,' said another.

As the 300 metres mark was passed, Eric heaved air into his lungs, willed his legs to move even more quickly, and pounded on and on, gaining speed! The American, whose burst had failed to succeed, saw only his rival's back as Eric Liddell swept through the tape 5 metres ahead of him, and smashed what was listed as the world record at the time!

Hundreds of Union Jacks and Scottish flags waved from side to side, and a cheer raised the roof of the stadium.

'Thank you! Thank you!' Eric breathed, to his heavenly Father.

Suddenly, a remarkably fresh athlete was surrounded.

'Congratulations!' Harold Abrahams laughed. 'That was amazing!'

'Great race!' 'Well done!' 'Amazing!' rang all around.

Newspaper reporters slapped him on the back, telling him what a wonderful guy he was. Some of them had torn him to shreds over the previous months. But that didn't matter to Eric. Nothing mattered to him except that he had kept God's law; he had kept Sunday special, and God had blessed him in a way he had never thought possible. The cheer that swept through the stadium when Eric received his gold medal rang on and on and on and on. And in the Flying Scotsman's brain, the prayer, 'Thank you! thank you! thank you!' nearly drowned it out.

It seemed as though Eric Liddell had a glittering career in athletics to look forward to. But none of his close friends were surprised when he told them that he was going to be a missionary, that he was going back to China where he had been born, and where he had the descendants of a certain billy goat to thank for his ability to run!

Eric Liddell married and became a father. His children had the same upbringing as he had, and in the same part of China. But by that time it was no longer a happy place, for China and Japan were fighting each other, and troops seemed to be everywhere. Li-Mu-Shi – that was Eric's Chinese name – tried his best to care for the Christians and to tell others about the Lord Jesus. He was a ray of light in a dark and fearful place.

The situation became so dangerous that Eric's wife and children were evacuated to Canada. Although he missed them hugely, Liddell must have thanked God that they were at last out of the war zone and safe.

'All British and American enemies report to Weihsien internment camp,' the Japanese soldier spat out.

Over the next three days they were taken, Eric among them, hundreds of miles to Weihsien and locked behind the high walls and electric fence of the camp.

'You can teach the children maths,' Liddell was told, when the prisoners tried to sort themselves into some sort of order.

'Uncle Eric' became one of the most popular men in the camp. And we can be sure that the children he taught learned more than maths from their Christian teacher.

Eric Liddell must have longed to see his own children again, but he never did. Desperately thin, dressed in rags and suffering from a brain tumour, the Flying Scotsman, who at the end could only stagger, died as a prisoner of war.

FACT FILE

The Olympics: The ancient Greeks held a series of Olympic Games at Olympia in Greece from 776 B.C. until the abolition of the Games in A.D. 393.

A French sportsman, Baron Pierre de Coubertin, had the idea of reviving the Games, and the first modern Olympics took place in 1896.

The Games have been held every four years since then, apart from 1916, 1940 and 1944 when they were cancelled because of the two world wars.

Keynote: Eric gave up the chance of an Olympic medal in the 100 metres because he knew that Sunday, God's day, should be kept special. Then he gave up a promising career in athletics to go to China and work for God.

Learn from how Eric always put Jesus first in everything, and remember that God said, 'Those that honour me, I will honour.'

Think: Do you have a favourite sport? Remember always to put Jesus first when you play any sport.

Look out for organisations that support Christians in sport. They can show you how to witness for Jesus by what you do and how you do it. They will also encourage you by telling you about other Christians who enjoy competitive sport.

Prayer: Lord Jesus, thank you for the sports I enjoy. Thank you for giving me the health and strength to enjoy them.

Make me a good witness for you as I play with my friends. Help me to put you first in everything. Amen.

William Carey

The boy shielded his candle with his hand and silently went into his bedroom. Several pairs of eyes reflected the light of the candle's flame. Two mice looked up at it from their box on the floor. Several birds stared, unblinking, from their cage made of willow withes. And there were tiny eyes too, so tiny that they couldn't be seen. There were crickets, woodlice, a number of spiders and a brown hairy caterpillar. William Carey had a bedroom to himself, but he shared it with as many animals and birds and insects as he could catch.

'I wonder what tigers are like,' the nine-year-old thought, as he pulled his rough blanket over his head. 'And zebras, they must look odd with all their stripes. But why do they have stripes? I'll have to think about that.' But he didn't, because he fell sound asleep and didn't waken up until the noise of mice, scratching in their box, broke through his dreams of faraway places, of jungles and wild animals, of brown-skinned people and pygmies.

Even after William had grown up, he was interested in faraway things. But, when he finished school aged fourteen, he only moved to a village a few miles from his home in Paulerspury, near Northampton, to learn to be a shoemaker.

Another teenager was also learning from the same master craftsman, and the two boys got on well although William, who had been brought up to know about the Lord Jesus, argued with the other boy because he was a Christian. William didn't think he needed a saviour, but what happened one Christmas made him really think about that.

'Would you like a sixpence or a shilling?' the ironmonger asked William, when he went into his shop.

William wondered what the catch was. A shilling was worth two sixpences – a lot of money to be offering a shoemaker's boy.

'A shilling, please,' he answered, not able to refuse the larger coin. And he had a great time spending some money on his way back to work. But the money he spent belonged to the shoemaker, and, when he went to replace it with his own shilling, he discovered it was a fake! The ironmonger had tricked him! He tried to lie his way out of trouble, but his boss found out. That experience made William Carey think. It was not too long afterwards that he became a Christian.

Over the following few years, there were many changes in Carey's life. He married Dorothy, and to support her and their children, as well as working as a shoemaker, he opened a little school. And at weekends he was a preacher.

'What are you doing?' Dorothy asked him one day. 'Whoever you're making that shoe for, has very funny feet.'

William smiled. 'Wait and see,' he teased.

Dorothy watched as he sewed strange shapes of leather together. And she was even more puzzled when her husband took out his ink pot, drew on the leather and then wrote words all over it! Only when it was finished, did William tell her what it was.

'It's a globe,' he announced, showing her the stuffed leather ball. 'And I've drawn on the countries and written in their names. This will help my pupils to learn what the world is like.'

'It's wonderful,' Dorothy said. 'There's India ... and Africa ... and Australia is right underneath.'

Perhaps William's pupils thought of other things they could have done with a leather ball, the size of a football!

William's interest in the world wasn't restricted to learning about animals and mountains, flowers and forests. He was most of all interested in people, and in telling them about the Lord Jesus Christ. That's why he was so eager to hear John Thomas speaking.

'Tell us about your work as a doctor in Bengal,' he urged Mr Thomas.

John Thomas was one of those people who couldn't stop speaking after he started.

William listened and listened, and, when the speaker eventually did stop, all William wanted to do was go home, pack up his clothes, and go to Bengal in India.

'No, no, no,' Dorothy insisted, when he made the suggestion later that evening. 'How can you even suggest we go to the other side of the world? We've got three little boys. The eldest is only eight, and there's another baby on the way!'

The months that followed were difficult for many reasons, but after the baby arrived, Dorothy agreed that the whole family could go to Bengal if her sister went with them to help. And that's what happened in 1793. John Thomas was on the same boat.

'Look at Father!' Carey's eldest son shouted, when he saw William on the deck of the boat one day. 'He's not got his wig on!'
'Did it blow away?' one of the other boys asked. 'Your head will get the shivers!'
All three boys went into such a fit of giggles that their mother, who was feeding the new baby, came to see what the noise was about. Her mouth fell open when she saw her husband!
William took a deep breath. 'I know I've worn my wig since my hair fell out years ago, but it's so hot and sticky and uncomfortable I decided to stop wearing it.'
'It was ugly too,' one of the boys said.
His father nodded. 'So it was.'

'Can we have it to play with?' two of his sons asked at once.

William shook his nearly bald head. 'I'm afraid not. I threw it into the sea.'

All three boys ran to the edge of the deck to look for it, but it had sunk without trace.

It took weeks to get to India, but the great day came when they saw that country for the very first time.

'Look!' William pointed to the far distance. 'That's our new home. That's India.'

The boys stayed on deck with their father as they drew closer and closer to land.

'Where do we go ashore?' one of William's sons asked.

'The boat goes to Calcutta,' Carey explained. 'But we are going to get off before that. A little boat will take us to Calcutta.'

'Why can't we go on this one?' he was asked.

'Because missionaries are not very welcome in India just now. If we were seen getting off, we might be sent all the way back home!'

That's how they came to be clambering down the side of the boat where the Hooghli river went into the sea.

After some months in India, the Careys moved inland to Mudnabatty where William was to work, and again they travelled by small boat.

'What's that?' 'What are they?' 'Look at that!' 'Wow!' 'This river smells!' 'There's a village!' 'The children haven't got any clothes on.' 'It's SO hot!'

The boys hardly stopped talking as they travelled, even though two of them had been really quite ill.

'Why's the river getting narrower?' one asked, a long time into the journey.

William pulled the child on to his knee. 'That's because we're in the jungle now.'

'Are there tigers here?'

'Yes,' William admitted. 'There are tigers.'

Dorothy looked at her husband. Her eyes seemed to be asking what on earth he was doing, taking them all to such a dangerous place. And she was positively cross when they arrived and discovered the house, they were to stay in, was already occupied! Thankfully, the Englishman who was living there, invited them to stay. In fact, he and Dorothy's sister fell in love and were eventually married.

'Hasn't God been good?' William said, after they had been in Mudnabatty a short time. 'I've a steady job working on the indigo estate, and that feeds and clothes us. I also have time to learn the language, so much so that I'll soon be able to preach to the people.'

Dorothy smiled. 'And to think that I didn't even know what indigo was before we left England. Now I know that its dye is what makes clothes a beautiful purply blue - indigo, in fact!'

'I'd never heard the word till we came here,' agreed Carey.

William was so good at languages that within a few months he had learned Bengali, written Bengali grammar, and translated parts of the Bible into the language too! And every Sunday he went preaching in the villages near where they lived.

Several things happened over the next while. Other missionaries came out from England to help with the work, and they were especially welcome as poor Dorothy Carey developed an illness that made her withdraw into herself.

In 1800, they all moved to Serampore where missionaries were welcome. A printing press was set up there to print the Bible and other Christian material in Bengali.

The missionaries all lived in one big house, though they did all have their own rooms.

'We need some house rules,' Carey said, when they had all settled down. 'Does anyone have any suggestions?'

'I think we should allow each other privacy,' someone said.

'Yes,' they agreed.

'After all,' one of the wives pointed out, 'We may be missionaries, but we are still human!'

'I have a suggestion,' a new member of the group said. 'I think we should meet every Saturday and settle any differences we've had that week.'

'What a good idea,' Carey enthused. 'Then we'll go into Sunday without any grudges or arguments.'

And that's what they did.

'Look at this!' was the excited cry, just three months after they had all moved to Serampore.

Everyone looked up.

'It's the first ever printed page of the New Testament in Bengali!'

'Praise the Lord!' Carey said.

That was a joyful day, and a very historic one too. But there were two problems: how were they to pay for printing materials? And how were they to distribute what they printed?

'Let's put an advertisement in the Calcutta newspaper,' Carey suggested, 'asking people who want parts of the Bible in Bengali to pay for them in advance.'

So many people answered the advertisement that there was enough money to keep on printing.

'Ow! Argh! Ouch!'

The screams came from outside the Serampore mission house. Carey and Thomas ran outside and found Krishna Pal, a Bengali carpenter, yelling with pain.

'His shoulder is dislocated,' Thomas said. 'We'll have to put it back in for him.'

As there was no anaesthetic, Krishna Pal was tied to a tree, and his shoulder was jerked back in.

The Bengali's screams changed. 'I'm a great sinner!' he cried. 'Krishna Pal is a great sinner.'

Thomas and William didn't think he understood what he was saying. But Krishna Pal did understand, and he was the first Bengali to become a Christian at Serampore. When Krishna Pal was baptised, so was William Carey's eldest son. A white English boy and a Bengali man were baptised together in the river.

In England, William Carey had been a schoolteacher, and he found himself doing the same thing in Serampore. Some of the missionaries there died, but those who were left, started a school. Nobody knows what Carey used as a globe, when he was teaching Bengali children about the world, but it may even have been another leather football!

FACT FILE
India: In 1498, Portuguese ships captained by Vasco da Gama, reached southern India, and European influence in India had its beginning.

British merchants knew that Indian goods – especially cotton cloth, drugs and dyestuffs (such as indigo) – fetched high prices in Europe.

In 1600, they set up the East India Company to organise trade. By 1757, it controlled the richest parts of India and almost all Indian trade.

Keynote: William answered God's call even when it took him and his family to the other side of the world to a country full of danger, where Christians weren't made welcome.

Learn from William's wholehearted commitment to Jesus even when it made life difficult. Ask God to give you the same commitment whatever happens in your life.

Think: Remember that there are still countries where Christian missionaries are not welcome.

Pray for Christian medical staff and aid workers in these countries. Pray that God would give them opportunities to share Jesus with the people they meet, without fear of injury or imprisonment.

Prayer: Lord Jesus, thank you for sending missionaries across the world. Keep them safe as they work for you.

Help me to be 100 per cent committed to you, even if it makes things difficult. Thank you for always being with me, no matter what. Amen.

David Livingstone

The foreman pushed David through the rows of clanking machinery, guiding him to John Purdie, cotton mill worker. When they reached him, the boy stood between the two men watching their faces as they spoke to each other. He couldn't hear a word over the noise of the machines, and he wondered how they could. Then it dawned on him, they weren't hearing at all, they were lip-reading. Nodding to David, the foreman left, checking each worker as he went down the long row. John Purdie crouched down to the boy's height, he wasn't tall for ten years old, and shouted into his ear.

'You copy what I do, and be quick about it. And watch your hands and your hair don't get caught in the machines!' he shouted.

David Livingstone nodded. He'd seen enough people in the village of Blantyre, where he lived, who had fingers missing, and bald patches on their heads where hair had been pulled out by the roots.

'Dad told me about that!' he shouted.

John Purdie looked puzzled.

'Dad told me!' the lad screamed, but his light voice was lost in the noise of the mill.

Purdie shrugged his shoulders and set to work.

David's first job was picking up the cotton dust from under the machine. Crawling on the floor with his head down, he grabbed handful after handful of the stuff, shoving it into a sack that seemed bottomless. It didn't matter how much he pressed in, it always seemed to be able to take more.

'Atchoo! Atchoo!' The dust caught in his nose, and when sneezing made him open his mouth, the stuff got into his throat, and he started to cough. Coughing made his eyes water, but, when he rubbed them, the fine fibres of dust on his hands found their way into his eyes. At last, his sack was full, and he crawled out from under the machine, guided by Purdie's pale-grey boots. Puzzled by their colour, David looked at himself and found that he was the same grey colour from head to toe.

John Purdie looked down and frowned, but not in an angry way. He had children himself, and he knew what the boy at his feet was going through. Taking a hankie from his pocket, he folded it into a triangle and tied it round David's face to stop him choking on the dust. 'He'll get used to it, poor boy,' Purdie thought. 'They all do.'

Taking David by the shoulder, Purdie pointed to the cotton threads on the loom, showing him how it held the threads in tight, straight lines, lifting alternate threads up and down with the action of the machine. Then he pointed to the shuttle that zipped forwards when one set of threads were up and backwards when the alternate threads rose. David watched, mesmerised by the up and down, backwards and forwards action of the vast machine.

Purdie suddenly jumped, and David saw immediately what had happened. One of the threads had snapped. In a flash, Purdie was under the machine to catch the loose thread then, grabbing the other loose end, he tied the two together and worked on. A nod of Purdie's head told David that was what he had to do. All week David worked hard with John Purdie, and by the end of the week he had learned to see broken threads, not so much by staring at the machine all the time, but by watching for the sudden jerk of a broken end.

'You've done well,' Mr Livingstone said, patting his son on the back that Saturday night. 'I'm proud of you.'

David smiled.

'And so am I,' his mum added. 'I'm just sorry you've got to work to help feed your wee brothers and sisters. But there will always be something for yourself,' she added, pressing some coins out of his first pay into the boy's hand.

David looked at the money. 'I know what I want to buy,' he said.

And what he bought with his very first pay was a book of Latin grammar! That book became well known in the mill, for the boy kept it propped up against his loom so that he could glance down at it and learn Latin grammar as he worked!

But the book David liked best of all was the Bible. His father read it with his family every evening, and much of Sunday was spent at church or reading God's Word. That suited the boy fine, because he believed in the Lord Jesus and wanted to find out more and more about him.

It was through his church that he heard about China, and how hard it was for the people there. Not only was there a terrible shortage of doctors in China, but most of the people there didn't know about the Lord. David decided to go to China as a missionary doctor - not easy for a poor mill boy.

David studied by day at his loom, and at night school too. Then he went to university for two years to learn some medicine. But, when he applied to go to China, there was a war going on there, and he found himself being sent to Africa instead.

In 1840, David sailed from London to South Africa via South America, a voyage which took many weeks. God had a surprise waiting for David. When he arrived, he went to work with another missionary, Robert Moffat. And Moffat's daughter, Mary, and David Livingstone fell in love and were eventually married.

'Why's that boy running so fast?' Mary asked one day.

David, who was treating a patient, looked up and saw a child racing for all he was worth toward the mission. Even from that distance, he could see his frightened expression. 'There's someone chasing him!'

'You finish this,' he said urgently, nodding towards his patient.

Livingstone ran, aiming to get between the child and the man who was chasing. The lad ran on, reaching Mary safely. The man slowed down, took in the situation, and slunk into the bush. But David wasn't going to let it finish there. 'What's wrong?' he demanded, when he cornered him.

'The boy, he ran away,' blurted out the breathless African.

David was pretty sure something fishy was going on.

'He's my son,' the man said. 'He tried to run away.'

But Livingstone recognised a lie when he heard one. In any case, the boy wasn't black like this man; he was brown; he was a bushboy. 'Wait there!' he ordered. The African, frightened by the stern Scot, sat down and waited.

'This lad's been sold as a slave!' Mary announced when he reached her. 'His parents are poor, and that rogue you've just caught bought him for next to nothing, and he's going to sell him for as much as he can get. The child will have no life at all if that happens. He'll just be worked to death!'

'Is this true?' Livingstone asked the terrified child.

And the whole story poured out, just as it had done to Mary. Suddenly, David's mind was not in Africa; it was back in Scotland, in the mill at Blantyre. He remembered how he had felt as a child labourer; he remembered the choking dust, his dry, cracked throat, and his red, running eyes. And he vowed to do whatever was in his power for Africa's child slaves. He, at least, had had loving parents; the poor boy at his feet had been sold to a rogue.

Suddenly, Livingstone remembered the man in the bush. He swung round ... but there was nobody there.

With terrific energy Livingstone threw himself into an amazing variety of work. He became a friend of the African people he met and did his best to understand them. His passion for preaching the good news of Jesus meant that he was always a student of the Bible and used every opportunity to preach to other people. But he didn't only care for their souls, he used his medical training to care for their sick and injured bodies too. And, as if that wasn't enough, he set out to explore Africa without the help of planes and helicopters, powered riverboats and quad bikes.

David and Mary loved young people, and God kindly gave them children of their own. How very sad he must have been, therefore, when his little family went home to Britain away from the diseases and troubles of Africa.

'I shall not see you again for a long time,' he wrote to his daughter Agnes, whom he often called Nannie, 'and I am very sorry. I have no Nannie now. I have given you back to Jesus, your friend, your Papa who is in heaven. He is above you, but he is always near you when we ask things from him - that is, praying to him - and if you do or say a naughty thing, ask him to pardon you, and bless you, and make you one of his children. Love Jesus much, for he loves you, and he came and died for you.'

Compared to Scotland, Africa is enormous, but David Livingstone set out to explore it, from top to bottom and from side to side.

'Apart from around the coast, Africa is all desert,' friends told him.

'It can't be,' he insisted. 'Look at the rivers that run into the sea. You don't get vast rivers in deserts!'

His friends shook their heads. 'But why do you want to go anyway?'

'There are people there who've never heard of Jesus,' David told them. 'There are tribes that haven't yet been discovered. There's a continent to explore.'

'There's no stopping him,' they decided, for his friends knew that exploring was one of his passions.

His journeys took ages because he travelled by ox-drawn cart or walked. And for very long periods of time, nobody knew where he was. There were no mobile phones in those days!

In 1867, David set off once again through Africa, exploring, map-making, and being a doctor and missionary all at once. His aim was to reach a place called Ujiji.

'What's that?' he asked the Africans who travelled with him to carry the luggage. They were known as bearers.

They turned their eyes away. They didn't want to see. Livingstone went over to look, only to find two bodies. And he knew from the marks on their wrists that they were slaves who had died as they were dragged to the slave ships.

'I must open up Africa,' he said to himself. 'I must. I must! It's the only way to stop this cruel trade in people.'

Through blistering sun and torrential rain they travelled, on and on and on. It took a year for them to reach central Africa.

'I want to divert a bit,' David Livingstone told his men, after looking at his compass for direction.

Black heads shook furiously. 'No!' some of his bearers said. 'We will never be home if you don't go straight to Ujiji. If you divert, we go home.'

The missionary explorer was torn. What should he do?

'How many of you will stay with me?' he asked.

Only five men agreed to go on with him, on a journey that saw them covered with leeches as they walked waist deep through rivers, torn by vicious thorns, bitten to distraction by mosquitoes, dodging crocodiles, and often putting their lives at risk. But still they went on, for a time carrying Livingstone who was ill for weeks. And their problems didn't end when they reached Ujiji. The supplies they had hoped to find there had been stolen.

The explorations of David Livingstone were by then very well known, and people in Britain, Canada, America and beyond had begun to think he had died in the middle of Africa. It was two years since news of him had reached home.

'I think we should run a story on Livingstone,' the editor of the New York Herald suggested to his staff.

'He's probably dead by now,' one man commented.

The editor nodded agreement. 'Dead or alive, that's not important. What's important is that we find out and publish the story. Would you be prepared to research this?' he asked a man called Stanley.

And that's how an American came to be in the interior of Africa looking for a Scotsman. And when he found him, Stanley held out his hand in greeting, saying, 'Dr Livingstone, I presume.' It could hardly have been anyone else!

FACT FILE
Cotton: A field of cotton ready for picking is covered with cotton balls. These balls are made up of soft, white fibres that are really pieces of very fine hair growing from the skin of many small seeds. The fibres have to be removed from the seeds before they can be spun into long pieces of thread or yarn. This separation process was done by hand.

Then, in 1793, Eli Whitney invented the cotton gin, which could be worked by one person and separate as much cotton as fifty to sixty people working by hand.

Keynote: David Livingstone saw Africa as a land full of people needing Jesus and vast areas waiting to be explored. He wasn't afraid to take on the challenge!

Learn from David's courage and his adventurous spirit. Remember that God is with you, too, so don't be afraid to take on a challenging task for him.

Think: Look up an atlas and compare the size of David's homeland, Scotland, with the vastness of Africa.

Isn't it amazing that God used a boy from a small town in Scotland to explore a continent the size of Africa? David's expeditions also brought a message of hope to people who had never heard about Jesus before.

Ask God to use you too, no matter where he takes you!

Prayer: Lord Jesus, thank you for men and women who have taken on big challenges for you.

Help me to look to you for strength and courage to deal with the challenges I face in my life today. Amen.

Nicky Cruz

Nicky hid under the back stairs of his home in Puerto Rico. No way did he want to see the people who were arriving. They were the snake people!

'Will your dad make them dance with snakes today?' his friend asked. 'I wanna see the snakes dance.'

Shuddering as he answered, Nicky said, 'You go watch. I'm heading off when the door shuts behind them. Papa'll beat me if he catches me watching in the window.'

'He wouldn't dare beat me,' the other boy boasted. 'My dad's the law here.'

Nicky chuckled. 'And what's the law compared to the witch doctor! I tell you, I'd rather be you than me. Do you think it's fun, everyone calling your home the witch's house?'

The door had closed. He started to run, stopped once and called out, 'You try it! You try living there! See how you like it!'

He was only ten years old, but Nicky Cruz thought he knew some terrible things. He was sure his mother hated him. Why else would she call him the devil's child. He knew he hated his father. And he hated anyone who bossed him around.

'Bully Cruz,' children shouted at him from a safe distance, and they were right.

'You'll either be murdered or be a murderer,' he was told more than once.

And when Nicky got a gun for killing birds, nobody came close. Nobody felt safe when he was around. Angry with everyone, he couldn't wait to get out of Puerto Rico; he couldn't wait to get to New York, the big city. Six of his older brothers were already there, and he was desperate for it to be his turn.

Eventually, at long last, the great day came. He turned his back on his family, aged fifteen, climbed on to a plane for the U.S.A., and hoped he'd never be back.

'Papa said to phone Frank when I arrive,' he said to himself. 'No way! I've had enough family to do me. I'll make my own way. Nobody will get the better of me!'

'It's freezing here,' Nicky decided, as he walked the city streets that night. 'But that looks hopeful.' He pulled a rag out of a dustbin. It was an ancient, buttonless, coat, but it felt like a blanket to the cold boy. 'One up to me!' he laughed.

But he wasn't laughing a day or two later as he sat huddled in a doorway.

'Wazzat!' He jumped, wiping hot tears away.

A mangy dog snuggled up beside him and licked his hand. The boy put his arms round the dog and wept ... until he noticed police boots in front of him.

In less than an hour, he was in Frank's flat and listening to a lecture. But Nicky knew in his heart that his brother's suggestion of school was not for him. He'd had enough of that in Puerto Rico. And before two months were out, the New York school Frank sent him to had had enough of him ... and his switchblade.

'Gimme that!' Nicky demanded.

The boy hesitated.

'Now!' The voice was menacing.

There was a click, his switchblade was open, open in front of the boy's face.

Dropping his money and the food he was carrying, the boy stumbled then half-ran, half-crawled, from the teenage madman with the blade.

Nicky picked up the wallet, grabbed an apple and sprinted away.

'No problem,' he said aloud, 'I can steal what I want, and, if anyone says "no" – he stroked his knife – I can persuade him.'

What Nicky Cruz didn't know was that he was being watched, but not by the police. The Mau Maus, one of New York's most vicious gangs, had their eye on him. He was just the kind of guy they were looking for.

Nicky was sixteen when he held his first revolver, and it felt good in his hands.

'You're our kind,' the gang leader told him. 'We can sure use you. You're a Mau Mau now, and there's no getting out. You're one of us - for good.'

Guns are just cold metal until they are fired. The first time Nicky fired his gun – and he fired it over and over and over again – was at a small boy in another gang. He was the most popular of all the Mau Maus after that fight, and he felt great.

It only took six months until Nicky Cruz was the Mau Mau president; that's how vicious he was. By then the police knew him well.

'I didn't do it, and I don't know anything about it!' he lied, about robberies, gang fights, assaults, drug raids, even murders.

The police knew he was guilty. Nicky knew he was guilty. But they could never pin anything on him. Although Nicky was popular with the gang, he wasn't always happy, especially at night when he had nightmares. For the next two years he was afraid to go to sleep. Nicky Cruz, the thug everyone feared, was scared of going to sleep.

It was summer 1958, and it was hot. Nicky and some other gang members sat at the edge of the street as young folk ran past.

'Coming to the circus?' one yelled.

Nicky looked up. 'What's going on?'

'There's a circus at the school,' the voice said, from the distance.

'We're going,' Nicky announced, and when Nicky announced something, everyone jumped to do it.

Outside the school a trumpeter played the same tune over and over and over again. Next to him was a skinny, weedy-looking man. Nicky could hardly believe his eyes. The trumpeter stopped, and the skinny guy climbed on to a stool and opened a book.

'Shout!' Nicky commanded. And the Mau Maus shouted, long and loud.

The man looked scared. He stood with his head bowed.

This was not Nicky's scene. Suddenly, the man wasn't the only one who was scared; Nicky Cruz was too.

When the crowd sensed the atmosphere, there was a tense silence. The man opened his book and read aloud, 'For God so loved the world that he gave his only son, that whoever believes in him, should not perish, but have everlasting life.' Then he went on talking to the quiet crowd of gang members. 'If you're so big and tough, you wouldn't be afraid of coming up here and shaking hands with a skinny preacher, would you?' he finished.

Some of the audience went up, shook hands, and got down on their knees right there in the street!

'They're showing you up, Nicky!' someone shouted.

His street cred was under threat. Nicky and his best friend marched to the front of the crowd, but when he reached the preacher, the young Puerto Rican didn't shake hands - he threatened to kill him.

'Jesus loves you,' the preacher said. 'Jesus loves you.'

The next day Dave Wilkerson, the preacher, found Nicky. 'I've just come to tell you that Jesus loves you. He really does.'

Nicky Cruz could have flattened him with one punch, and both knew it.

'One day, you'll stop running,' Wilkerson said, 'and you'll come running to Jesus.'

And that's how it was. Nicky did stop running, and he did come to Jesus. But what is much more amazing than that, is that Jesus wanted him to come. Jesus loved Nicky Cruz even though he had done unspeakable things. Jesus wanted to forgive him.

'I won't need this again,' thought Nicky, as he shoved his Mau Mau jacket in a bag. 'Things are going to be different.'

The gang was waiting for him, waiting to see what was going to happen. They had all been there when Nicky Cruz said in public that he was going to follow Jesus.

'Right, you lot,' their president told the Mau Maus, 'get your guns, blades and bullets and meet me in Washington Park.'

The gang relaxed. Everything was just as usual.

'We're gonna march to the police station and hand them over.'

They looked at each other, then at Nicky. But his look was like cold steel. They did exactly as they were told, much to the amazement of the police who thought it was some kind of trick!

'I want you to go to Bible School,' Dave Wilkerson told the new Christian before much time had passed. 'That gets you out of New York, and God's got plans for you at Bible School.'

'School.' Nicky was even allergic to the word! But he went, only to discover he was like a fish out of water. His English was poor; as a Puerto Rican he was a native Spanish speaker. He didn't know how to behave. And when he was told to do something, his instinct was to do the opposite. He tried to fit in. Nicky really, really tried, but it was such hard work. God helped him though, and he especially helped him by allowing him to fall in love. Gloria was also at Bible School, and they set out together to see what God wanted them to do with their lives.

'Hey Dave,' Nicky Cruz said into the phone. 'I've got news for you.'

Dave Wilkerson groaned. It was evening where Nicky was, but the middle of the night with Dave! 'Can't it wait till morning?'

'No! I'm calling to tell you I'm coming to work with you in New York for the summer.'

That wakened Dave. 'That's great! That's really great!'

And it was. Some of Nicky's old friends from the Mau Maus recognised him, even though he was clean and wearing different clothes. They listened to what he had to tell them about Jesus, and some became Christians.

At the beginning of that summer, Nicky had news for Dave; at the end, Dave had news for him.

'Someone has given me money to send you on a trip home to Puerto Rico to see your folks.'

Nicky swallowed hard. Since he'd become a Christian, he'd really wanted to see them again. He'd no hate in his heart for them any more. The trip was arranged, and he set off. While he was in Puerto Rico, Nicky was asked to preach. And at the end of the service, when he asked anyone who wanted to become a Christian to come to the front, his own mother moved forward, knelt down and asked Jesus to be her Saviour.

'I'm enjoying school so much better this year,' Nicky told Gloria, after returning from New York and his visit home. 'Now that I know God can use me, I can see the point of studying.'

Because of that, the year passed quickly. It didn't seem like several months later when a letter arrived from Dave Wilkerson.

'Gloria!' Nicky yelled, when he read it. 'Dave wants me to go back to New York when I finish, to Teen Challenge Centre, to work with gangs and addicts and drunks, people just like I used to be. But I'll be carrying a Bible instead of a revolver or a switchblade.'

The girl watched his excitement. 'Yes,' she thought, 'that's just what Nicky's cut out for. That's just the work God has spent all these years preparing him to do.'

Nicky Cruz moved back to New York, and he and Gloria were married. The work they did through Teen Challenge was tough. They were working with the hardest of all young folk. They had great sorrows when gang fights led to murders, when kids died of drug overdoses, when some took their own lives. And they had tremendous joys when others kicked their drug habit, quit their fighting, left gang life behind them and followed Jesus.

FACT FILE
New York:
New York lies on the Atlantic coast of America, at the mouth of the Hudson River.

Every traveller, entering or leaving New York harbour, sees the great Statue of Liberty on Liberty Island. The statue, made by F. A. Bartholdi, was given to the United States by France in 1886.

Another feature of New York is the great collection of skyscrapers which tower over Manhattan, in the heart of the city.

Keynote: Nicky's family life taught him to hate, and his time in a New York gang encouraged this anger into violence. Love was something that Nicky had never experienced.

Learn from how the love of Jesus broke through the hatred in Nicky's heart and completely changed his life. Believe that the love of Jesus can do the same today too!

Think: Maybe there's a bully in your school - someone who is rebellious and angry and doesn't care about hurting others. Think of the impact there would be if the bully's heart was full of love for God, instead of hatred towards others!

Focus on praying for that person. Pray that God will change bullies, and believe that he can do it.

 Prayer: Lord Jesus, thank you for loving us so much that you died for us.

Help me to show your love, not just to my friends, but also to those whom I feel are my enemies. Use me to bring the message of your love and forgiveness to them too. Amen.

Adoniram Judson

Two pigs snuffled around the boy's feet, as he emptied the scraps from his little bucket into their trough. Then the maid poured in a much larger pail of food.

'Listen to them!' she laughed, as she picked the child up out of reach of the mess. 'I'm glad you don't make a noise like that when you're eating!'

Three-year-old Adoniram laughed. 'Piggies speak with their mouths full,' he said. 'They say "shlurp, shlurp".'

'What does the cockerel say then?'

The child grinned. He loved the cockerel. 'Cockadoodledoo!' he crowed.

'You are a clever little boy,' the maid said, as they picked their way through the mud at the back of the house and up the path to the kitchen door.

'Master Adoniram knows all the animal sounds now,' the maid told Mrs Judson, the child's mother.

Mrs Judson smiled. 'And he says them all with your Boston accent.'

'It's the best accent in all of America!' the girl said. 'And it's the one all his little friends will have when he goes to school.'

'On the subject of school, Adoniram,' his mother said, 'let's you and me go through to the parlour. There's something I'd like us to do.'

Mrs Judson sat down on her rocking chair, pulled her son on to her knee, and opened her big Bible.

The child looked confused. 'Is it bedtime?' he asked, knowing that his mother or father always read him a Bible story before he went to bed.

Smiling at the thought, Mrs Judson explained that she read the Bible a number of times each day as well as at bedtime.

'That's good,' said Adoniram, 'cos I'm not sleepy.'

Then a thought crossed his mind. 'Mama, why does Papa have to go away so often?'

'He has to go away to preach,' she explained, 'to tell people about the Lord Jesus.'

Adoniram knew about preaching, because his father was a minister.

'Would you like to give Papa a surprise when he comes home next week?' Mrs Judson asked the little boy.

'What surprise?'

His mother opened the Bible. 'Let's see if we can teach you to read for Papa.'

She pointed to a word. 'That says God, and the three letters are G - o - d. Can you see anywhere else on the page that says God?'

Adoniram searched over the page of print. 'There!' he said triumphantly, 'and there! and there!'

'Well done!' laughed his mother. 'You can read a word already, and such an important word. Now let's find another one.'

She pointed to the page. 'That word says Jesus, and the five letters are J - e - s - u - s. Can you see anywhere else it says Jesus?'

It took him a minute, but the lad found the word Jesus.

'I like this game,' he said.

A week later, a very excited little boy watched at the window for his father.

'Papa! Papa!' he shouted, when he saw him coming. 'Come and see the surprise.'

Rev Adoniram Judson, tired after a long journey, took off his coat, sat down on his chair and pulled his son on to his knee.

'You have a weary papa,' he said, 'but you make up for me. You're so full of energy.'

'May I show you my surprise?' the child begged. 'It's in the parlour.'

Adoniram told his papa to sit by the fire. The boy sat down in his own little chair, and his mother handed him the Bible open at the place. Then Adoniram Judson read a whole chapter to his amazed papa! The words were read quite slowly, but correctly. Only when he had finished reading did the child look up.

'Why are you crying, Papa?' he asked, shocked at his father's response.

Rev Adoniram Judson hoisted his son on to his knee and hugged him close. 'These are not sad tears,' he explained. 'These are happy tears, very happy tears. Who taught you to read the Bible?'

Mrs Judson was grinning.

'Mama did,' the child explained. 'She said I could learn to read a chapter when you were away for a week, and I did.'

'And you've made me the happiest father in Boston. And the most amazed. What a clever boy you are. And what better book to read than the Bible.'

'It's my favouritest book,' the child said, stroking its leather cover.

By the time he went to Master Dodge's School, some time around 1786, he had read much of the Bible for himself.

'Let's play churches,' Adoniram suggested to his little brother and sister some years later, when they were old enough to play with him. Their mother smiled from her seat by the fire.

The two younger children sat down. They liked this game because it meant a lot of noisy singing.

Adoniram opened his Bible in the middle, and read, 'I have hidden your word in my heart.'

'Mama,' he said. 'Why would anyone want to hide God's Word, even in their heart?'

Mrs Judson thought for a moment. 'It doesn't mean it's all hidden away and forgotten about; it means that you love it so much that you learn it by heart and remember it. Do you understand?'

The boy nodded, but it still seemed to him a strange idea to hide a Bible.

Years later, the little boy, who had liked playing at preachers, was a real preacher, and not in America, but on the other side of the world, in the Buddhist country of Burma.

He and his wife, Ann, were missionaries. But there were problems, big problems in Burma's Golden City, because the Burmese were fighting the English.

'The situation is getting desperate,' Adoniram said. 'Rangoon has fallen to the British, and we're being suspected as spies.'

'But we're not British!' insisted Ann.

'But we're white, we speak English, and we're not Buddhists. That's more than enough to make us suspects.'

There was loud banging at the door of the mission house. Adoniram rose to answer, but it was shoved open in his face.

Ann turned deadly white. It was the spotted faces!

'You're under arrest!' they told Judson, tying his elbows together behind his back.

Ann struggled to reach her husband but was held back by the Burmese Christian who lived with them.

After Judson was hauled out the door, the little group in the mission house stood in stunned silence. Then all the questions came at once.

'Where will they take him?'

'Will they torture him?'

'The spotted faces ... they're the most feared of the guards.'

'They're all former criminals.'

'They're all still criminals.'

The Burmese Christian, Judson's first convert, led the little group in prayer. That evening, Ann, with the help of her friends, burned any papers in English. But one big pile of papers was not burned; it was buried in the space under the mission house.

'Death Prison!' Ann Judson gasped. 'They've taken Adoniram to Death Prison.' She shuddered, thinking of all the terrible things that went on there. Straightening her back, she looked at her friends. 'We have to be brave,' she said. 'And we have to take food every day to Death Prison. The guards don't feed the prisoners, so we must.'

Each day, rice, wrapped in leaves, was taken to the prison, but often whoever took it, didn't tell Ann all that they had seen and heard. Sometimes, the prisoners were strung upside down, with only their shoulders on the floor, all night. They were beaten and tortured in dreadful ways.

'Take this to Adoniram,' Ann told her Burmese friend one day. 'He needs a pillow.'

She handed him a brown, cloth pillow. It wasn't soft and fluffy; it was hard and lumpy. And Adoniram's heart rejoiced, even in Death Prison, when he got the uncomfortable pillow.

Many months after Adoniram was imprisoned, there was frightening news.

'They're not in Death Prison!' the Burmese Christian said, as he came in the door. 'They've been moved away.'

A shudder ran round the room. Had they been moved away, or had they ...?

Ann, who had only recently had a baby and was still very weak, went to visit an important lady in the city who would be able to tell her if it was good news or bad. The news was not good, but it was better than it might have been.

'All the white prisoners have been moved to Amarapura,' she told her friends, when she came back. 'We'll need to go there to feed Adoniram and the others.'

The little group, including baby Maria, were bundled up and taken by boat to Amarapura, near where they found the prisoners in a derelict jail.

'My pillow,' Adoniram said sadly to his wife; 'I wasn't able to bring my pillow with me. All my work is lost, all my years of work.'

Only Ann Judson understood what his pillow meant to him.

That night, Adoniram Judson prayed and prayed. His pillow was lost. And he and his fellow prisoners, whose feet had been locked in stocks, were again hanging upside down with only their shoulders on the ground. His heart wept in prayer for the people of Burma.

Shortly afterwards, a new prisoner arrived, a huge and hungry lioness in a cage!

'What's she here for?' the chief guard demanded.

'Maybe the prisoners have to be fed to her!' another guard suggested.

And that's what all the prisoners thought too.

Things seemed to be at their very worst when two things happened. The lioness died, and soldiers came with news that the prisoners had to be released and taken back to the Golden City. The King of Burma needed them because they spoke English. The war with England was over, and he needed English speakers to negotiate the peace treaty.

What a welcome the pathetic little group got when they arrived back in the mission house in Golden City.

'How did you come to be here?' Mr Judson asked a teenage boy who seemed to be living there. His father, though not a missionary, had been in prison with Judson.

The boy told his story, and he ended it by saying that he'd gone to Death Prison to see his father the day the prisoners were taken away. In his distress, he had looked for something to remind him of his father and had found Mr Judson's pillow. And he had discovered its secret!

Adoniram Judson had translated the New Testament into Burmese, and when it looked as though it might be destroyed, Ann buried it. Then she dug it up, sewed it into a pillow, and sent it to her husband in prison.

'Praise the Lord!' Adoniram, weak and exhausted, was nearly dancing his thanks to God. 'Praise the Lord!'

The boy had more to tell. 'When I discovered it was a book,' he said, 'I read it. I read all about Jesus, and I became a Christian.'

Adoniram Judson had preached the gospel in Burma for years with only one or two people coming to faith. But God used his terrible time in Death Prison to turn a teenager from a Buddhist into a believer in the Lord Jesus Christ.

FACT FILE

Memory: How good is your memory? Some people find it easier to remember things by picturing them in their mind's eye, as if they were taking a mental photograph. Others have good memories for sounds and tunes. Some try to remember things by repeating them quietly to themselves.

However weak your memory might be, you can make up for it by listening carefully to what you want to remember and repeating it over and over again.

Keynote: Years later, in a Burmese prison, Adoniram would thank God that as a little boy he had memorised so many Bible verses. He knew that these verses were stored in his memory forever and would help him through his ordeal.

Learn from how Adoniram drew comfort from God's Word and try memorising some key Bible verses yourself. You never know when you might need them!

Think: Did you know that, even today, many Christians are imprisoned because of their faith? Thank God for how freely we can worship him and live as Christians.

Don't forget to pray for those whose freedom has been lost and whose lives are at risk because of their love for Jesus.

 Prayer: Lord Jesus, thank you for your Word and for everything it tells me. Help me to treasure it more.

Be with Christians around the world who are in prison because of their love for you. Bless them with your presence and care in a special way. Amen.

George Müller

George stomped about the room, only just resisting the thought of kicking the table leg as he went past. He was in a rotten mood, and he didn't care who knew it.

'I want to go out to play football,' the boy moaned.

George's father looked stern. 'You can go out after you've done your accounts.'

His son stamped his feet. 'It's not fair!' he said. 'None of my friends have to write down how they spend their pocket money.'

Herr Müller was cross. 'You'll sit down and do what I tell you. And I'm telling you that you've to keep a note of how you spend every single penny you get. I'll be back in five minutes to see what you've done.'

Herr Müller shut the door behind him.

George took out his notebook and screwed his face into a scowl. Then he wrote down that he had spent that week's pocket money on a pencil, rubber and a notebook. The boy sat back and grinned. 'He'll never find out that I really lost it on a bet.'

The door handle rattled, and Herr Müller came back in. George handed his father the notebook.

'That's good,' he told his son. 'I'm glad you don't waste your money. You know,' he went on, 'because I'm a taxman for the Prussian government, I know a lot about what people do with their money, and so many just spend it on rubbish. They think I don't know, but I do.'

'May I go out to play now?' the boy asked. He didn't want to hear any more about his father's work, and he didn't want to hear any more about money either.

'I wish I had some sweets,' George thought the next day. 'But I haven't any money to buy them. I lost all this week's pocket money on that bet!'

Then he noticed the money his father had gathered in taxes. It was in a box with a lock, but the key was in the lock. Looking round to make sure nobody was coming, he opened the box and took out some money.

'Where can I put it?' he asked himself.

Then he had an idea. Taking off his shoe, he slipped the coins into it and put it back on again. He was only just in time because his father came into the room.

Herr Müller sat down at his desk, opened the money box and started to count what was in it. George walked quietly towards the door.

'Come here!' barked his father.

The nine-year-old boy did what he was told.

'Have you taken anything out of this box?'

George tried to look shocked. 'Me!' he said. 'I didn't go anywhere near it!'

'Take off your jacket,' Herr Müller told his son firmly.

George took it off.

His father checked the pockets, but there was no money there. Then he searched George, but found nothing.

'Now take off your shoes,' he told the boy.

George took them off very, very carefully.

'What was that?' the man demanded, when he heard the chink of coins.

The lad ducked to avoid his father's slap. But he wasn't quick enough.

'I left the key in that box deliberately,' Herr Müller said, 'because I was quite sure you were stealing from me, and I wanted to double-check. Don't you ever, ever do anything like that again. It's a terrible thing when a father can't trust his son with money.'

Instead of getting better, George went from bad to worse. He left home as soon as he possibly could, got into bad company, and by the time he was sixteen, in 1821, he was in prison for dishonesty. Several times he tried to be good, but it always went wrong, and he ended up worse than ever. Then a friend of George's became a Christian. In desperation, George asked his friend if he could go with him to a Christian meeting at the home of Herr Wagner.

'Come in,' Herr Wagner said, opening the door wide. 'Welcome to my home and my heart.'

The other boy went first because he knew the way.

'That's a nice welcome,' thought George, as he took off his coat. He began to relax in the roomful of people.

'What on earth's he doing?' Müller asked himself.

They had just sung a hymn, and now one of the men was kneeling down and praying.

George had never seen such a thing before! In Prussia, at that time, people used prayers out of books. Nobody made up their own prayer in public. It was unheard of.

Müller looked at the kneeling man and listened.

'It's as though he's speaking to a king,' he thought.

After praying, the man read the Bible and preached a sermon. George was amazed! The man was breaking the law! Only men ordained by the church were allowed to preach. So shocked was the youth that he listened to every word that was said.

Something happened in George's heart during that meeting. He not only met men and women who were friends of Jesus, he met the Lord Jesus himself. He didn't see him with his eyes or hear him speak, but his heart knew that God was present in that room. By the time George left Herr Wagner's meeting, he had asked God to forgive his sin.

'I challenge you to a drinking match,' one of his student friends said a few days later.

George looked at the group of young men. They were all drinkers and gamblers as he had been.

'No,' he said, 'I'm not coming. I'm a Christian now.'

The group all stopped speaking. Then one grinned.

'A Christian! We'll see about that. I bet you're back in the pub tomorrow.'

They turned and swaggered away, leaving George looking at their backs. He didn't go with them that day, and he never went with them again.

'We need missionaries,' a preacher said one day, when Müller was back at Herr Wagner's house. 'We need people who will tell others about the Lord Jesus.'

George stared at the man. 'A missionary?' he thought to himself. 'I wonder ....'

God did call George Müller to be a missionary, which is why he moved to London where he worked for a time with Jewish people. And it was in England that he met the young woman he married. Eventually, the Müllers and George's friend, Henry Craik, moved to Bristol to be joint ministers of a church there. But soon after they arrived, cholera struck the city, and many people died, leaving hundreds of children hungry and homeless. George and

Henry opened a small orphan home, then another, then a third.

Some years later, God led them to build a huge new home just outside the city, at Ashley Down. Amazingly, a second home was built there, and a third one too! Over the years Müller and Craik worked together; they provided a home, food, clothes and education for over two thousand children. Never once did they ask anyone for a penny. They took all their needs to God in prayer, and they had some spectacular answers.

The matron of the infants' home went to Müller one day.

'I don't have money for the milk we need,' she explained.

George took the money box out of his desk and counted what was in it. They were two pence short of what was needed.

'Let's pray about it,' he said.

They prayed that the Lord would provide money for milk for the infants. When George opened the door to let the matron out, a poor woman stood there.

'I don't have much money,' she told him, 'but the Lord led me to bring this to you.'

She handed over two pence, exactly what was needed for the milk.

Some time later, the children thought it was just an ordinary day. But it wasn't. They did their schoolwork and finished their chores, not knowing that there wasn't enough food for their dinner. The staff in the home knew, and they also knew that there was no money to buy what was needed. Suppertime came nearer. The children were ready for their meal, and the staff prayed with all their hearts. God answered their prayers. Just as they all sat down to say grace, the baker arrived at the door to ask if they could use some bread! He had made more than he needed and had plenty to spare! The children gave thanks and ate their meal, never thinking that God had provided it that very minute. In all the years the homes ran, no child ever went hungry.

'The heating boiler isn't working,' an assistant at the home told George one winter day. 'There's a serious leak.'

'But it's so cold, and we can't have the children chilled,' Müller said to the man. 'How long would it take to get a new boiler?'

'A month,' was the reply.

George and his wife prayed about it and felt that they should get someone else to come and investigate the problem. But that would mean putting the boiler out and letting the children get cold.

'We'll pray that God will change this freezing north wind to a warm south wind the day the boiler's off,' they agreed. And that was their prayer.

On the day the workmen came, the cold north wind turned to the south and blew mild and warm! The following day, it was freezing again!

'Where does the money come from to run these huge housefuls of children?' a visitor to Ashley Down once asked.

'It comes from the Lord,' George Müller answered.

His visitor looked puzzled. 'Tell me what you mean.'

George stood up, went to the window, and looked out. The children were playing, hundreds of them. Each was dressed in neat, good quality clothes and shoes. The girls had nice haircuts. And they had balls to play football with and dolls to cuddle.

'I mean that the Lord miraculously provides every single penny. We receive no grants and accept no loans. We don't send begging letters, and we don't make appeals for funds. We don't tell people what we need, and we don't tell them we have bills to pay.'

The visitor watched Müller's face as he talked. Although he was eighty years old, he looked as excited as a child.

'What we do is this. We get down on our knees, and we tell the Lord all about it, and he has never, ever failed to answer our prayers. We receive gifts of food and material for clothes. Some people arrive at the door and give us pennies, others come with hundreds of pounds. Over the years we've run the homes, we've been given in money or kind over a million pounds. And remember, we've never asked for a penny.'

'Mr Müller,' the visitor said, 'that's an amazing story. But may I ask you one last question?'

The old man smiled and nodded. 'What's that?'

'What was your training before you were a minister? Were you an accountant? You certainly seem gifted in handling money.'

George Müller wondered how much he should say to this man, and decided to tell him all.

'My training in accountancy was carried out by my father before I was ten years old. And as for being gifted with money, before I became a Christian, I was a gifted young thief.'

FACT FILE

Napoleon: Napoleon was a Corsican soldier (originally known as Napoleon Bonaparte) who became Emperor of France in 1804, the year before George was born.

Napoleon set out to conquer Europe, but, after victories at Austerlitz and Jena, he made the fatal mistake of invading Russia in 1812. He reached Moscow, but lost many men in the severe winter cold.

In 1813, Napoleon was defeated, and he abdicated the following year. After returning to rule France for 100 days in 1815, Napoleon was finally completely defeated in the Battle of Waterloo. He spent the rest of his life in exile.

Keynote: George depended on God for everything. He knew that if he shared his needs with God, he could be sure that everything would be taken care of. He had absolute trust in God, and the Lord never let him down.

Learn from how George handed over all his needs to God in prayer and trust him to take care of you too.

Think: When you pray, remember to:
- thank God for everything he's given you.
- tell him about what you need, not what you want. There's a difference!
- give God the glory when your needs are met.

 Prayer: Lord Jesus, thank you for how you have answered my prayers in the past.

Help me to trust in you more and always to bring my needs to you first. Make me more and more dependent on you every day. Amen.

Luis Palau

Luis and his sister Matil crouched under the canvas sheet that was covering their father's bags of cement.

'What's that?!' Luis jumped.

'Shhhhh...' Matil whispered. 'It's Dad's belt. We've had it now!'

The pair huddled together. It had seemed a good game to pretend to run away from home. But it had turned sour on them. Both knew what the jingle of their dad's belt meant.

'Come out of there the pair of you!' Mr Palau's voice said, right above their heads.

First Luis crept out, dusty and shamefaced. Then came Matil who was already in tears.

'Bend over,' their father ordered. And both did.

Tea that night was not comfortable for two reasons. Mr Palau's long prayer before they ate, seemed to have more to do with asking forgiveness for sin than for thanking God for their tea, and two bottoms were not very comfortable for sitting on.

Although Mr Palau was strict, he loved his children very much, and they knew it. One of the things that young Luis really liked doing, was creeping into his father's study first thing in the morning. He knew that he would find his father there, wrapped up in a poncho to keep himself warm in the chill of the Argentinian morning, and praying. Luis loved hearing his father praying for him and for the rest of the family. Somehow, he felt that as long as his father was wrapped in his poncho and praying each morning, everything would be all right. He might get rows, he might even be beaten with his father's belt, if he was especially naughty, but everything would end up all right.

'Now that you're seven,' Mr Palau said to his son, 'you're old enough to go to boarding school. What do you think of that?'

Luis didn't know what to think. He would have to stay in a dormitory with other boys. He would miss his family.

'Will there be midnight feasts?' he asked.

His father laughed. 'There might be sometimes.'

'It'll be brilliant!' the boy enthused, trying to sound keen. 'But I'll miss you.'

'And we'll miss you, big boy,' Mr Palau said, hugging him. 'But we'll be praying for you, and you'll be praying for us. God will keep us close.'

'Dear Mum and Dad,' Luis wrote, after a few days at boarding school. 'I miss you. I cried under the covers last night. Please let me come home.' Then he tore the page out of his pad and started again. 'Dear Mum and Dad, I'm sharing a dormitory with other boys. Some of them are nice, and I'll be friends with them. Please write and please send me a parcel.'

But he soon became used to boarding school and began to enjoy it. Every month he went home for a weekend. And that's how his life was for nearly three years.

'There's a message for you, Luis,' a teacher told the ten-year-old. 'Come to the phone, please.'

'Luis!' the voice said. 'It's your grandmother here. I've news for you. Your father is very ill, and we have to pray for him.'

The boy's head spun, and he felt suddenly sick. What if this was serious? What if his dad was really bad? What if he died?

'I'll get a train ticket for you,' his grandmother went on. 'And you'll go home tomorrow. Your mom wants you home.'

Luis didn't sleep much. He tossed and turned all night, thinking about his father.

The train journey home lasted three hours, but for Luis it lasted forever. 'Go faster ... go faster ...' he told the train. 'Get me home. I need to be home.'

The train eventually stopped at the station, and the boy jumped off and bolted home. Fear made him race to get there, and fear made him want not to be there at all.

'Why does God allow this?' he heard his aunt say, as he reached the door.

Then another voice. 'So many little children left without a father.'

Suddenly, it was as though Luis's heart wasn't there. There was just a cold space inside him. Racing past relatives who tried to grab him, the boy only stopped when he came to his father lying in bed, dead.

It was 1944. Luis was ten, but suddenly he was a man, a little man with a broken heart.

It was a very sad Luis Palau who went off some months later to start his secondary education at another boarding school. And his first year there wasn't very happy.

'I know Dad's gone to heaven,' he would say to comfort himself. 'But I don't know if that's where I'll go.' He was in a muddle, not knowing what to believe. In bed at night, he sometimes tried to put into words what was happening in his heart.

'I want to be a Christian, but I like things Christians shouldn't like. I want to go to heaven to be with Dad, but I'm not sure if I want to be different from my friends.' And from time to time he would fall asleep saying over and over to himself, 'I don't know what I want. I just don't know.'

At the end of his first year in secondary school, Luis went to a Christian camp, and there he discovered that Jesus was who he needed and who he wanted. When he went home from camp, it was with good news for his mother. He was a Christian.

'Luis!' she said, cuddling him close enough to take his breath away. 'Luis, I've not been as happy since your dad died.' Tears rolled down her cheeks, tears of pure joy. 'You've made me the happiest mum in Argentina!'

There were many ups and downs in Luis Palau's life after that, but God had a plan for him. And when God has a plan, he works it out exactly.

When Luis Palau was in his twenties, he was a preacher, but he realised how few people went to church compared to the vast numbers who didn't.

'Why can't we hire a sports stadium and fill it with people?' he asked his Christian friends.

'Because they would come for baseball, but not for a sermon,' one said.

Luis insisted. 'They go to hear Billy Graham ... hundreds of thousands of them. The more I think about it, the more I'm convinced that's how to reach people. They won't come to church, but they might come to a stadium.'

'That's all you talk about, Luis,' a friend complained. 'You're setting your sights too high.'

Luis Palau looked him in the eye. 'Are you telling me God's not able to do it?'

There was no answer to that.

'Give me a hug, son,' sighed Mrs Palau, as she and Luis said goodbye.

'I'm only going to America to Bible School,' he said, holding her close. 'It's not exactly outer space.'

And when he was in America, he married Pat, and they set out to serve God together for the rest of their lives.

In the years that followed, Luis's dream of huge crowds gathering to hear the gospel, began to come true. And since he started preaching, it's estimated that over six hundred thousand people have said, at Luis Palau crusades, that they would like to become Christians.

Palau didn't only speak to people at huge meetings, he also gave regular live broadcasts on television and radio. And it was on the morning, after one television broadcast, that three people arrived at the door.

'Will you come in?' Luis said to the woman and two burly men.

The woman entered. 'One of them will stand outside the door, the other at the gate,' she announced.

Before she sat down, she looked into all the corners of the room and checked behind a picture! Suddenly, she let fly with twenty minutes of abuse about Christianity.

Luis looked at her as she spoke, but he was praying rather than listening to the terrible things she was saying.

'How can I help you?' he asked eventually, when she stopped for breath.

The woman sank into her chair, suddenly sobbing fit to burst.

'You're the first person ever to offer to help me,' she wept.

Luis smiled gently. 'What's your name?'

'Why do you want my name?' barked the woman.

'Just because I don't know what to call you.'

She relaxed a little and gave her name. Immediately, Palau realised she was from a hugely wealthy family.

'I'm a Communist,' she said. 'I don't believe in God. But I'm going to tell you my story. I ran away from a religious family, then married and divorced three times. After I became a Communist leader, I organised student rebellions, demonstrations and uprisings.'

Nearly three hours later, she was still going strong, then, as suddenly as she started, she stopped.

'Supposing there's a God – and I'm not saying there is – would he have anything to do with a woman like me?' she asked, after a pause.

Luis opened his Bible.

'I don't believe the Bible,' she snapped.

'You're supposing there's a God,' Palau said quickly. 'Then let's suppose this is his Word. It says here that God doesn't remember the sins of those who trust in him.'

'But I've committed adultery. I've been married three times.'

Quietly, Luis repeated what he'd said. 'God doesn't remember their sins.'

'I've stabbed a comrade who later committed suicide.'

'God doesn't remember their sins.'

'I've led riots where people have been killed.'

'God doesn't remember their sins.'

Seventeen times, the woman told of terrible things she'd done. Seventeen times, Luis reminded her that God would not remember her sins if she trusted in him.

Finally, she sighed. 'Well,' she said. 'It would be a miracle if he could forgive me.'

And with that she left with her bodyguards.

Two months later, Luis was back in that woman's city in Ecuador and went to see her. When she opened the door, he was shocked at what he saw. She stood there, covered in bruises and with several teeth missing.

'What's happened?' he gasped.

The woman explained. 'I'm no longer an atheist,' she said. 'I believe in Jesus. But when I told my comrades and resigned from the Party, they tried to run me down with a jeep, then they attacked me and smashed my face until I was unconscious.'

There was a Communist revolution planned for some months after that woman's attack. On the morning the revolution was to start, the Party leader came to talk to her, just a few hours before it was planned that he would take over as ruler of Ecuador.

'Why did you become a Christian?' he asked.

She explained how Jesus had changed her life.

'I've been listening to that programme on the radio,' he said. 'And it almost has me believing in God.'

'Why don't you?' the woman urged. 'Why don't you think about it?'

And he did.

Later than morning, what was supposed to be a revolution, fizzled into chaos, and Ecuador was saved from a bloodbath.

Becoming a Christian means change. All who have become Christians, through Luis Palau's crusades, have had their hearts changed. Some have changed their lifestyles, others their aims and ambitions. And a few, like that woman, have changed the future of a country.

FACT FILE
Ecuador: Ecuador is a country of huge volcanoes, deep valleys, swampy coastlands and exotic wildlife.

There are humming-birds, brilliantly coloured finches, parrots, antbirds and flycatchers. Mountain animals include alpacas and llamas. Monkeys, tapirs, jaguars, pumas, caymans and boa constrictors live in the rainforests. Strange fish, like the plated catfish and the volcano fish, swim in the mountain rivers.

Keynote: Luis's heart was broken when his father died. His father was in heaven, and Luis wanted to be sure that he would get there too. Luis was worried about what his friends would think, but he knew that he needed Jesus in his life.

Learn from how Luis didn't just follow the crowd. Being a Christian would make him different from his friends, but he would have Jesus as his best friend - forever!

Think: God doesn't remember the sins of those who trust him.

We're not as forgiving when someone lets us down, are we? Sometimes we even enjoy reminding that person about where they went wrong. It makes us feel better about ourselves!

Ask God to change your heart, so that you bear no grudges and are willing to forgive.

Prayer: Lord Jesus, thank you for reminding me that you don't remember the sins of those who trust in you.

Take away any bitterness in my heart towards people who have hurt me. Make me willing to forgive them instead. Amen.

QUIZ

How much can you remember
about the ten boys who
changed the world?

Try answering these questions
to find out ...

BROTHER ANDREW

1. What injury left Brother Andrew crippled?

2. What did Brother Andrew smuggle behind the Iron Curtain?

3. What wall came down when Communism ended in eastern Europe?

JOHN NEWTON

4. How did the mayors of harbour towns sometimes supply the press gangs with the men they needed?

5. John Newton left the navy and joined a merchant ship, *Pegasus*. What was that ship's cargo?

6. What job did John take on when he ended his life at sea?

BILLY GRAHAM

7. Billy Graham was born in the same year as the end of which war?

8. Where did Billy go when he was nineteen years old?

9. What subject divided America in the 1960s?

ERIC LIDDELL

10. Eric Liddell ran in the 1924 Olympics. Where were they held?

11. Eric's father had been a missionary in which country?

12. Eric won his gold medal in which race?

WILLIAM CAREY

13. What did William Carey do when he left school?

14. What did William Carey use as a globe?

15. William worked on an estate that produced a purple dye. What was the name of that dye?

DAVID LIVINGSTONE

16. Where did David Livingstone work as a boy?

17. David went as a missionary to Africa, but where had he originally applied to go?

18. Which newspaper sent Mr Stanley out to Africa to find Livingstone?

NICKY CRUZ

19. Where was Nicky Cruz from?

20. What was the name of the New York gang that Nicky joined?

21. Which member of Nicky's family became a Christian after Nicky preached in Puerto Rico for the first time?

ADONIRAM JUDSON

22. Where did Adoniram Judson go as a missionary?

23. What was hidden in Adoniram's pillow?

24. What was the name of the prison that Adoniram was taken to?

GEORGE MÜLLER

25. Where did George Müller hide the money he had stolen from his father?

26. George opened children's homes in which English city?

27. What was the name of the large, new children's home that was opened on the outskirts of the city?

LUIS PALAU

28. Where was Luis Palau from?

29. How old was Luis when his father died?

30. Through the woman who trusted in Jesus, after speaking to Luis, a Communist revolution was prevented in which country?

How well did you do?

Turn over to find out ...

ANSWERS

1. A bullet went through his ankle.
2. Bibles, Christian books and tracts.
3. The Berlin Wall.

4. They emptied the prisons.
5. Slaves.
6. A minister.

7. The First World War.
8. To Bible School.
9. The subject of race.

10. Paris.
11. China.
12. The 400 metres.

13. A shoemaker.
14. A stuffed leather ball.
15. Indigo.

16. A cotton mill.
17. China.
18. The New York Herald.

19. Puerto Rico.
20. The Mau Maus.
21. His mother.
22. Burma.
23. The New Testament in Burmese.
24. Death Prison.

25. In his shoe.
26. Bristol.
27. Ashley Down.

28. Argentina.
29. Ten years old.
30. Ecuador.

Start collecting this series now!

Ten Boys who used their Talents:
ISBN 978-1-84550-146-4
Paul Brand, Ghillean Prance, C.S.Lewis,
C.T. Studd, Wilfred Grenfell, J.S. Bach,
James Clerk Maxwell, Samuel Morse,
George Washington Carver, John Bunyan.

Ten Girls who used their Talents:
ISBN 978-1-84550-147-1
Helen Roseveare, Maureen McKenna,
Anne Lawson, Harriet Beecher Stowe,
Sarah Edwards, Selina Countess of Huntingdon, Mildred Cable,
Katie Ann MacKinnon,
Patricia St. John, Mary Verghese.

Ten Boys who Changed the World:
ISBN 978-1-85792-579-1
David Livingstone, Billy Graham, Brother Andrew,
John Newton, William Carey, George Müller,
Nicky Cruz, Eric Liddell, Luis Palau,
Adoniram Judson.

Ten Girls who Changed the World:
ISBN 978-1-85792-649-1
Corrie Ten Boom, Mary Slessor,
Joni Eareckson Tada, Isobel Kuhn,
Amy Carmichael, Elizabeth Fry, Evelyn Brand, Gladys Aylward,
Catherine Booth, Jackie Pullinger.

Ten Boys who Made a Difference:
ISBN 978-1-85792-775-7
Augustine of Hippo, Jan Hus, Martin Luther,
Ulrich Zwingli, William Tyndale, Hugh Latimer,
John Calvin, John Knox, Lord Shaftesbury,
Thomas Chalmers.

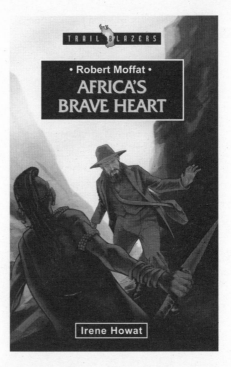

Robert Moffat, Africa's Brave Heart
by Irene Howat
ISBN 978-1-84550-715-2

The story of a Scottish minister and his wife in Africa – the precursors to David Livingstone. With a sword, a shovel, a Bible, and great courage, Robert used the skills he had learned growing up in a Scottish village to translate the Bible into Tswana and to share God's love with Africa.

OTHER BOOKS IN THE TRAILBLAZERS SERIES

The Adventures Series

Have you ever wanted to visit the rainforest? Have you ever longed to sail down the Amazon river? Would you just love to go on Safari in Africa? Well these books can help you imagine that you are actually there.

Pioneer missionaries retell their amazing adventures and encounters with animals and nature. In the Amazon you will discover Tree Frogs, Piranha Fish and electric eels. In the Rainforest you will be amazed at the Armadillo and the Toucan. In the blistering heat of the African Savannah you will come across Lions and elephants and hyenas. And you will discover how God is at work in these amazing environments.

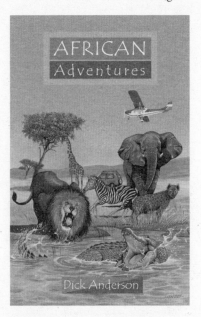

ISBN: 978-1-85792-807-5

The Ivan
Series

Ivan and the Informer
Ivan is at a secret Bible study but when he leaves the Secret Police are waiting outside. Find out how Ivan tackles the police and some false accusations.

ISBN 978-1-84550-134-1

Ivan and the Hidden Bible
Ivan and Katya are at the Lenin Collective Farm to help with the harvest. There is a hidden Bible on the farm. Can they find it?

ISBN 978-1-84550-133-4

Ivan and the Secret in the Suitcase
Ivan has been asked to take part in a dangerous mission. While on holiday Ivan has to have a secret meeting and pick up a suitcase. But what is in the suitcase? And will the Secret Police find out?

ISBN 978-1-84550-136-5

Ivan and the Daring Escape

Ivan's friend Pyotr has been kidnapped. How will Ivan help his friend to get back home? Find out how Ivan outwits the Secret Police once again!

ISBN 978-1-84550-132-7

Ivan and the Moscow Circus

Ivan and Katya meet Volodia, a trapeze artist with the Moscow Circus. Volodia's uncle is in prison for criticizing the communist government. Can anything be done to help him?

ISBN 978-1-84550-135-8

Ivan and the American Journey

Ivan has won a trip to America. But what will he do when he discovers there is a defector in their group? Should he help or should he just walk away?

ISBN 978-1-84550-131-0

CHRISTIAN FOCUS PUBLICATIONS

Christian Focus Publications publishes books for adults and children under its four main imprints: Christian Focus, CF4K, Mentor and Christian Heritage. Our books reflect our conviction that God's Word is reliable and Jesus is the way to know him, and live for ever with him.

Our children's publication list includes a Sunday School curriculum that covers pre-school to early teens, and puzzle and activity books. We also publish personal and family devotional titles, biographies and inspirational stories that children will love.

If you are looking for quality Bible teaching for children then we have an excellent range of Bible stories and age-specific theological books.

From pre-school board books to teenage apologetics, we have it covered!

Find us at our web page:
www.christianfocus.com

CF4 •K
*Because you're never
too young to know Jesus*